The Gardener's Wise Words and Country Ways

To my sister Lois and brother Richard, who have both made wonderful gardens in distant continents.

The Gardener's Wise Words and Country Ways

Ruth Binney

D&C
David and Charles

A DAVID & CHARLES BOOK
Copyright © David & Charles Limited 2007

David & Charles is an F+W Publications Inc. company
4700 East Galbraith Road
Cincinnati, OH 45236

First published in the UK in 2007

Text copyright © Ruth Binney 2007
Illustrations copyright © David & Charles 2007

Ruth Binney has asserted her right to be identified as author of this work
in accordance with the Copyright, Designs and Patents Act, 1988.

A catalogue record for this book is available from the British Library.

ISBN: 978-0-7153-2583-4
ISBN: 0-7153-2583-3

Printed in Great Britain by Antony Rowe
for David & Charles
Brunel House, Newton Abbot, Devon

Commissioning Editor: Neil Baber
Assistant Editor: Louise Clark
Senior Designer: Sarah Clark
Production Controller: Beverley Richardson

Visit our website at www.davidandcharles.co.uk

David & Charles books are available from all good bookshops;
alternatively you can contact our Orderline on 0870 9908222 or write
to us at FREEPOST EX2 110, D&C Direct, Newton Abbot, TQ12 4ZZ
(no stamp required UK only); US customers call 800-289-0963 and
Canadian customers call 800-840-5220.

CONTENTS

INTRODUCTION

Every gardener, however inexperienced, has wisdom to share. I have been lucky enough to be the recipient of a great deal, and it is my love of gardens and plants, and my fascination with old-fashioned adages and advice, that have been the driving forces behind this book. Many of my earliest memories are of helping my father in the garden – starting with simple jobs such as deadheading dahlias and picking raspberries – and it was he who made the first contributions to my collection of sayings, including 'Plant potatoes on Good Friday' and, to predict the weather, 'Oak before ash, only a splash'. Being a scientist, he was also keen to test every saying against the reality of each year's gardening successes and failures, and I feel that in writing this book I am doing no more than carrying on his legacy.

Although it is an old saying that I have only recently discovered for myself, my father would most definitely have approved of the notion that 'To be a good gardener one must be well acquainted with geology, entomology and meteorology – as well as with botany, chemistry, drawing and colour'. It is this multidisciplinary approach that makes gardening so appealing, plus, of course, the pleasure that comes from the physical acts of hoeing, weeding and pruning, the joy of having flowers indoors and out, and the immense pleasure of cooking and eating fruit and vegetables minute-fresh from the plot.

It is probably not surprising that many well-worn sayings and pieces of advice about the garden relate to old-fashioned cottage garden flowers like roses, carnations and sweet peas, to perennially favourite vegetables such as peas, potatoes and beans, and to the essentials of garden practice, including digging, raking and lawn mowing. The sayings and quotations I have chosen to include in this book strongly reflect this emphasis. Many famous gardening names are here, such as Vita Sackville-West, Robert Thompson and William Robinson, but also many lesser-known people whose advice and observations live on in their prose and poetry. And as well as recording what gardeners of times past recommended – and what works today – I have also tried to convey the emotions that gardens and gardening have evoked and offer glimpses of the garden in mythology, folklore and superstition.

As in my previous books, including of course the original *Wise Words and Country Ways*, the research for this modest volume of gardening lore and practical advice has involved the pleasure of searching bookshops and second-hand stalls for old volumes and of making use of the wide selection on offer at the London Library. Although neither my flower garden nor my allotment is ever – and probably never will be – free of slugs or weeds, I have managed not to let writing interfere too much with my passion for being outdoors among the plants. My special thanks are due, as ever, to my tolerant husband Donald (also lawn cutter, manure shifter and ace weeder), and to my daughter Laura for her encouragement. I am also indebted to Neil Baber and his team at David & Charles and to Beverley Jollands for her meticulous editing.

It was Gertrude Jekyll who wrote that 'The love of gardening is a seed that once sown never dies', a sentiment with which I heartily concur. I hope that you enjoy reading this book as much as I have enjoyed its writing.

Ruth Binney
West Stafford, Dorset, 2007

1. THE JOYS OF THE GARDEN

'You are closest to God in the garden' – or so the old saying goes, and there are few keen gardeners who would dispute this fact. In its very origins the garden evolved as a place of perfection, a kind of paradise designed to revive both body and soul. Elements of this idea live on today, and to the passionate gardener, whether religious or not, there is no more pleasurable way to spend a day than digging, planting, pruning – or just pottering around the garden.

Just the sheer physical work of gardening can do wonders for your wellbeing (as long as you take care not to strain your back), since exercise produces in the body 'feel-good' chemicals called endorphins. Equally, there is great pleasure to be had in planning what you are going to grow and in choosing and ordering plants, bulbs and seeds. And although it is simply a fact of nature's inevitable cycle, there is something hugely exciting about seeing the first bulbs of spring pushing up through the ground and spotting the first snowdrop or daffodil. Equally thrilling is the magic of the germination of plants from tiny seeds carefully planted and, as summer and autumn progress, the opening of fragrant blooms and the harvest of crops – to enjoy freshly picked with family and friends and to preserve and store for the winter.

HE WHO PLANTS A GARDEN PLANTS HAPPINESS

And health, too. For those who love both plants and physical activity there is no better combination, although gardening can be notoriously bad for the back.

Gardening lifts the mood, like any other physical activity. But even the sights and smells of a garden can raise the spirits. It is also proven that physical activity is a healthy way of dealing with stress, which will help to prevent dangerous rises in blood pressure. So it is perfectly legitimate to indulge in 'secateur therapy' or to dig or weed yourself to a better state of mind. If you are both vegetable gardener and cook, a straight line to happiness is drawn by harvesting vegetables and, within minutes, making them into a delicious meal that you have created yourself and know to be additive free.

The idea is not new. Advising gentlemen 'which have little else to do', William Coles in *The Art of Simpling* of 1656 states that they should '… spend their spare time in their Gardens; either in digging, setting, weeding or the like, than which there is no better way in the world to preserve health'. As well as health of the body, Coles also considered gardening a worthy diversion from 'idleness, and evill company, which often times prove the ruine of many ingenious people'.

'What greater pleasure can there be than to smell the sweet odour of herbes, trees, and fruites, and to behold the goodly colour of the same …'

(Leonard Mascall, 1572)

You're closest to God in the garden

A version of a sentiment expressed in the poem *God's Garden* by Dorothy Frances Gurney, and a reflection of the link between the garden and paradise.

Whatever one's feelings about religion, it is undeniable that the making and tending of a garden can lift the spirits and produce genuine feelings of wonder and admiration at the beauty of nature. The usefulness of the garden is also a marvel, and it is surely no accident that, like medieval monks, we increasingly cultivate herbs for their medicinal and cosmetic – as well as their culinary – uses.

The book of Genesis describes the role of divine intervention in the creation of the garden: 'And the Lord God planted a garden eastward in Eden … And out of the ground made the Lord God to grow every tree that is pleasant to the sight, and good for food …' and Gurney embroidered this account in her poem, which begins:

The Lord God planted a garden
In the first white days of the world,
And He set there an angel warden
In a garment of light enfurled.

And ends:

The kiss of the sun for pardon,
The song of the birds for mirth, –
One is nearer God's heart in a garden
Than anywhere else on earth.

Though the ancient Egyptians were probably the earliest gardeners, it was their export of the notion of gardening to Persia that turned the garden into a place of pleasure. Paira-daeza was the Persian name for a terraced park planted with trees and shrubs and encompassing a game reserve. Most famous of all the ancient gardens were the Hanging Gardens of Babylon – one of the seven wonders of the ancient world.

PLANT FOR PLEASURE WHERE YOU WALK OR TREAD

An old saying that is best taken as an instruction for placing perfumed plants where they can be most appreciated. Even a lawn can bring pleasure to the senses.

Alongside paths, plan for scents that will stimulate the senses all year round. In spring, there are few bulbs that beat narcissi for perfume, notably the pheasant's eye or poet's narcissus (*N. poeticus*), whose pale cream petals surround a flat, central corona, edged in red. More headily fragrant is the hyacinth, which is ideally planted beneath roses. Lavenders are also ideal edging plants. Select from both the traditional hardy lavenders such as the strongly scented *Lavandula angustifolia*, and the more tender French lavenders like *L. stoechas* 'Papillon', the butterfly lavender (see also page 125).

An evening walk through a summer garden is hugely enhanced by the scents of night-scented stocks (*Matthiola longipetala* syn. *M. bicornis*), whose blooms open only at dusk. These hardy annuals make excellent pot plants. Another wonderfully fragrant evening opener is the tobacco plant (*Nicotiana alata*), whose cultivars include the unusual 'Lime Green'.

Where you tread, try planting thymes between paving stones or plunged beneath gravel. Even the slightest crushing of their leaves will waft a wonderful smell to the nostrils. Or plant an old-fashioned chamomile lawn, using the non-flowering Chamaemelum nobile 'Treneague', whose feathery leaves release a strong apple-like scent when crushed.

It is said that the lavender gained its heavenly scent when the Virgin Mary laid the swaddling clothes of the infant Jesus over it to dry.

For winter scent, three outstanding scented shrubs are worth a place by any path. Daphnes, including the easy and reliable *D. x napolitana*, whose pink flowers are surrounded by deep green leaves; *Sarcococca hookeriana*, the Christmas or sweet box, with its clusters

of small, cream blooms; and any of a number of winter-flowering viburnums. An excellent one is *V. farreri*, with tubular pale pink flowers.

AN OLD TOOL IS A GARDENER'S COMFORT

All gardeners have their favourite tools, which perfectly fit the hand and the stature. Whatever the tool, it always pays to buy the best and maintain it with care, so that it works well and lasts for years.

The fork, spade, trowel, hoe, rake and shears, the essentials of the modern gardener's tool shed, evolved largely from farming implements – the original shears, for instance, were used for removing wool from sheep. But with advances in technology, and the increasing popularity of gardening, specific gardening tools were developed. Secateurs with curved blades, for instance, specifically for rose pruning, were first made in France in 1818 as gardening became more widespread.

Never buy a tool without first holding it in your hand or trying it in action to be sure that it feels comfortable and of the correct weight. Wood – traditionally ash or beech with a smooth, straight grain – still makes the best handles, staying cool and dry in your hands.

In 1687 the English landowner and intellectual John Evelyn compiled a list of 100 'Tooles & Instruments Necessary for a Gardiner &c.' ranging from 'Three spades of severall sizes' and '3 Rakes of several sizes & finenesse' to '1 bird clapper ... 1 Turf beater' and 'Beehives of all sizes'.

A SHARP TOOL IS A GOOD TOOL

And so is a clean one. When you come in from the garden after a day's work, even if you are exhausted it is worth taking the time to clean up your tools and to keep them sharp and free of disease-spreading organisms.

Before they can be sharpened effectively, tools need to be free of rust. Remove it by brushing with a wire brush, then wipe blades with an oil-soaked rag. If you are going to sharpen tools yourself, your sharpening stone first needs to be treated with a few drops of oil. The accepted routine for any straight blade is to push it against the stone, both forwards and to the side. The blade then needs to be turned over and moved almost flat against the stone, to remove any rough edges. For blades such as shears and secateurs it is often easier to move the stone rather than the blade. Once the tool is sharp, a light application of oil is recommended.

TIPS FOR KEEPING TOOLS IN TRIM
- *Use a stiff brush to get excess dirt or oil off tools.*
- *Sprinkle the cut surface of half an onion with caster sugar and rub it on tool blades.*
- *Rub secateur blades with methylated spirits after use to stop them harbouring disease.*
- *'Feed' wooden handles with linseed oil before you put tools away for the winter.*
- *Clean the teeth of a saw with an old toothbrush.*

Old newspaper is good for getting dirt off spades and forks. In his *Gardener's Assistant* (1859), Robert Thompson also recommended an 'implement cleaner', which was 'a small wooden spatula ... indispensable in working adhesive soils, where tools become clogged. It may be formed out of a bit of thin deal by the workman, and of any form that he may prefer.'

THE ANSWER LIES IN THE SOIL

A gardening truism, for all good gardeners not only need to know their soil, and the plants that will thrive in it, but also have to work continually to maintain the soil in tip-top condition.

The soil in which gardens grow is formed, essentially, from rocks on the earth's surface, which have been crumbled by wind and weather and mixed with the decayed remains of plant and animal life: plants exist and thrive on the remains of their dead predecessors and competitors. The basic nature of your soil is determined by where you live, though there is much you can do to improve it.

'I think the answer lies in the soil' was the catchphrase of the character Arthur Fallowfield, who was played by Kenneth Williams in the 1960s British hit radio comedy *Round the Horne*.

For gardeners, the ideal soil is loam – midway between sand and clay, enriched with vegetable matter. A good loam will be water retentive and well drained and, when dug and raked, will slip easily through the fingers. Taking cues from such perfection, the key to improving soil is to dig in vegetable matter, or even – if texture is your problem – shredded newspapers.

In the flower garden, the plants that will do well will depend on whether your soil is acid or alkaline. As well as azaleas and rhododendrons, camellias, magnolias, kalmias and pieris all love acid soil, as do fruits such as blueberries and cranberries. If your soil is more acid than you would wish, the best treatment is to incorporate ground chalk or limestone and to favour spent mushroom compost, which contains large amounts of lime. Alkaline soils, by contrast, are ideal for alpines such as saxifrages and pinks, for alliums and cyclamens and for the cultivated varieties of chalkland species such as scabious and campanula.

LOVE A WORM

Earthworms are invaluable because except in the depths of winter they work the soil, helping to produce a fine tilth. Even wormcasts, brushed over, will help to improve a lawn.

Eating worms is an act of bravado but also a metaphor for misery, as in the children's rhyme: 'Nobody loves me, Everybody hates me, I'm going down the garden to eat worms.'

'The earth without worms,' said the renowned naturalist Gilbert White, 'would soon become cold, hard-bound and void of fermentation, and consequently sterile.' He was right, for worms are nature's ploughmen, loosening, rotating and aerating the soil and carrying digested organic material down into it. To encourage worms, keep your soil moist and dig in extra leaf mould or shredded newspapers.

Charles Darwin made a detailed study of worms' habits and behaviour, even tempting them to devour pieces of raw meat. He estimated that there are about 53,000 earthworms in every acre (0.4 ha) of soil. 'In many parts of England,' he calculated, 'a weight of more than ten tons of dry earth annually passes through their bodies and is brought to the surface on each acre of land; so that the whole superficial bed of vegetable mould passes through their bodies in the course of every few years.' Earthworms, he concluded, had played an 'important part in the history of the world'.

Earthworms most familiar to the gardener are *Lumbricus terrestris*, known in some parts of the world as the nightcrawler, and those of the genus *Allolobophora*, which make their casts on lawns. In a compost heap, the best worms to encourage are red brandlings (*Eisenia fetida*).

WORMS TO AVOID
Not all garden worms are benign. These are some that are less than welcome:
Wireworms – *tunnel into potatoes and carrots.*
Eelworms – *attack bulbs, making them discolour and rot, stunting and distorting leaves.*
Cutworms – *devour the leaves and shoots of lettuces, brassicas and young annuals.*

NIMBLE FINGERS MAKE FOR BEST TRANSPLANTING

This is certainly true if you are transferring seedlings. All young plants need a gentle touch when being pricked out, to avoid damage to their leaves and roots.

Tugging at young plants is an easy way to damage them. Much better is to ease them out of the soil with a small fork, the sharpened end of a pencil or a 'mini trowel' with a pointed end. Another good way to avoid damage, ideal for long-rooted seedlings such as peas and beans, is to grow them in hinged cells

or 'root trainers', which can simply be opened out to remove the seedlings.

Timing is critical, too. As John Coutts, curator of Kew Gardens in the 1920s and 1930s advised, it '... should always be done at the earliest possible moment. Delay in thinning and transplanting means that the seedlings become drawn-up and weakly; when they are eventually moved the fibrous roots become torn and the seedlings will take much longer to become established. They will, in fact, never make such sturdy plants as those transplanted at the right time.'

GREEN-FINGERED TIPS FROM OLD GARDENERS

- *Wait until it rains – the seedlings will then get maximum water.*
- *Transplant in the evening – plants will recover best in the cool of the night.*
- *Firm small plants in place, but do not trample them as this may damage the roots.*
- *Make a hole for each plant with a dibber or trowel that is just the right size, to avoid a parching air pocket beneath the roots.*
- *Transplant seedlings of all sizes, especially when growing mixed colours of flowers. In stocks, for example, you are more likely to get doubles from small seedlings.*

SEEDS AND CUTTINGS CAN BE HAD FOR THE ASKING

A tribute to the undoubted generosity of gardeners – and nature's abundance. It is a rare gardener who likes to waste spare seed or seedlings, or begrudges a cutting for a neighbour from a favourite plant.

Seeds may not always be exactly the gift you were expecting. If gathered from hybrid plants they may not come 'true'. Equally, cuttings taken from plants grafted on to a different rootstock may produce plants that are very different in size from those of the giver.

A GARDEN THAT IS NOT BEAUTIFULLY NEAT IS NOTHING

But a garden that is too neat and tidy will be no help to wildlife, which can work greatly to a gardener's advantage.

Neat is great if it means regular deadheading, removal of decaying and discoloured leaves and shoots and keeping the garden free of weeds. A neat garden will also have its plants staked so that the wind does not blow them flat. And while over-tidy planting can risk a 'municipal park' look, a parterre planted with formal box hedging looks ghastly if not kept neatly clipped.

The advantages of wildlife in the garden are many. A pile of bark or old logs is a perfect winter home for beetles, frogs, toads, hedgehogs and many other animals that helpfully devour slugs, snails and other pests. Stones, as well as fallen leaves and branches, are excellent habitats for the millipedes, centipedes, woodlice and other invertebrates that help recycle garden debris and turn it into compost. And a woodpile or an undisturbed corner of a shed is a choice hibernation site for butterflies.

COUNTRY-STYLE GARDENING

The cottage garden is the triumph of informality over neatness, though it can be just as much work for the gardener as a more rigid design. Describing her own garden in 1832, Mary Russell Mitford conjured up a quintessential cottage plot: 'The house, granary, wall, and paling, are covered with vines, cherry trees, roses, honeysuckles, and jessamines, with great clusters of tall hollyhocks running up between them; a large elder overhanging the little gate, and a magnificent bay-tree …'

THE FREQUENCY OF CUTTING, NOT THE SHORTNESS OF THE GRASS, PREVENTS AN UNTIDY LAWN

An exhortation to get out the lawnmower, and set its blades at a height appropriate to both the degree of growth and the weather. Mowing the grass neatens the whole garden.

A newly mown lawn, with edges neatly clipped, is the epitome of outdoor tidiness. Mowing needs to be most frequent in spring when the grass is growing most strongly. This helps to thicken growth and reduce the sprouting of weeds and moss. Be aware of the weather. In prolonged dry spells leave the grass longer, and in mild years be prepared to carry on mowing late into autumn. Be even more reluctant to mow in times of drought; there is more shame in wasting water watering your lawn than in having a brown sward. It will revive in a few days once rain finally falls.

The first cut of the season can be crucial. As Francis Hadfield Farthing explained in his 1929 manual, '… The wise gardener adopts a policy of moderation at this juncture. He does not set the blades of the machine too low or cut too closely. The temptation to adopt this course, in the mistaken belief that it will ensure a fine surface quickly, is one that should be avoided. Too close cutting will merely expose the roots of the young finer grasses to drying winds and bursts of hot spring sunshine with possibly disastrous results.'

Grass is easily killed off if you walk on it after a heavy frost, so why doesn't mowing grass hurt it? It is because the growing tips lie beneath the soil

> 'Nothing is more pleasant to the eye than green grass kept finely shorn.'
> (Francis Bacon, 1625)

and are not damaged by cutting (or nibbling by herbivores). It is this fact that lies behind the vital role that grass plays in nature's food web, sustaining grazing animals by the million all over the world.

> The traditional English lawn evolved from the Tudor bowling alley, and by the 17th century it was a distinctive garden feature. Men with scythes kept the grass short until 1830, when Edward Budding invented the lawnmower. The Gloucestershire textile engineer ingeniously adapted a machine he had created for cutting the nap on woollen cloth. Other 19th-century gardeners, such as John Rae, demonstrated the importance of rolling in creating lawns as fine and even as good carpets.

A GARDEN PATH MUST HAVE A PURPOSE

To form an approach to the house, to lead from one part of a garden to another, or to allow plants in the garden to be appreciated to the full. The character of a path will depend on both the materials you choose and its route.

Writing in 1904 about Compton Wynyates in Warwickshire, one of England's most venerable Tudor houses, Gertrude Jekyll described to perfection the essentials of paths in one of the house's smaller gardens, highlighting the use of grass paths. 'Straight along it is a broad grass walk with flower borders on both sides, leading to a thatched summer-house that looks out upon the moat. Lesser paths lead across and around among vegetables and old fruit-trees … The space within the quadrangle of the building is turfed and has cross-paths paved with stone flags. Bushes of hardy Fuchsia mark their outer angles of intersection.'

On the more modest scale of most domestic gardens, interest and an illusion of space can be created by avoiding straight paths. Winding paths combined with steps work well, and both brick and gravel (in which plants can be sited or encouraged to overlap) are excellent materials, easy on both the eye and the feet. Across a lawn, individual pieces of stone can be laid, sunk so that the mower glides over them, to add interest and avoid undue wear to the grass, especially in winter.

THE ITALIAN GARDEN DOES NOT EXIST FOR ITS FLOWERS

An acute observation from the American novelist Edith Wharton, and a valid expression of the nature of gardens whose design is a result of both history and climate.

Even in the Tuscan hills, the heat of the Italian summer makes cultivation of any but the most drought-tolerant plants a practical impossibility, which is why evergreens and stonework are the essential ingredients of the Italian garden, and have been so since the Renaissance. Cypress groves, arbours and topiary are also key elements, and many gardens originally incorporated caves or grottoes. Pools and fountains were also often included to enliven the sombre greens.

Symmetry is another key element of the formal Italian Renaissance garden, which commonly extended in a semicircle in front of the house. As Edith Wharton

(1862–1937) explained: 'Intricacy of detail, complicated groupings of terraces, fountains, labyrinths and porticoes, are found in sites where there is no great sweep of the landscape attuning the eye to larger impressions.'

THE WIDER PICTURE

As in other parts of the world, the development of the Italian garden was linked with the landscaping of grounds extending around a country house or villa. The best garden design adapts to the architecture and setting of the house but also accommodates the landscape, setting paths to run through managed woodland, planting orchards around the perimeter of the formal garden and framing distant views.

EVEN AN UGLY WALL MAY BECOME A SWEET GARDEN

Either by accident or design, plant seeds will germinate in the crevices of walls, covering them with a delightful selection of blooms. Or they can be deliberately planted to enhance your boundaries.

Two very common wall growers, which will 'take' without any intervention from the gardener, are *Corydalis* (usually the yellow *C. cheilanthifolia*) and the red valerian (*Centranthus ruber*). For deliberate decoration, choose alyssums, aubretias and moss campions (*Silene acaulis*) for a sunny wall; for shade, plant arabis, the ivy-leaved toadflax (*Cymbalaria muralis*) and varieties of rosette-forming saxifrage such as *Saxifraga paniculata*. To keep young wall-sown plants in place and prevent them from being washed out by the rain, anchor them in place with small pieces of modelling clay, shaped to fit around their necks.

FAST CLIMBERS

For quick camouflage for an ugly wall there are many attractive climbers and ramblers to choose from, quite apart from the cliché ivies and Virginia creepers. Solanums will scramble rapidly in sheltered spots, while 'Danse du Feu' and *Rosa filipes* 'Kiftsgate' are two fast-growing roses. Any *Clematis montana* will also make a quick cover for an unsightly boundary.

The wallflower, *Erysimum (Chieranthus) cheiri*, though more usually planted as spring bedding, can still be found in some country places growing on old walls.

HOURS FLY, FLOWERS DIE

The start of a poetic sundial motto, and a vivid reminder of the effects of time on the garden. The sundial was once a garden necessity, sometimes constructed from plants.

This motto appears around the sundial in the garden at Yaddo, an artists' retreat in Saratoga Springs, New York, founded in 1900 by the financier Spencer Trask and his wife Katrina, a poet. At the base of the gnomon is another verse, by their friend Henry Van Dyke:

In full, the motto reads:
'Hours fly,
Flowers die,
New days,
New ways,
Pass by;
Love stays.'

Time is
Too slow for those who wait,
Too swift for those who fear,
Too long for those who grieve,
Too short for those who rejoice;
But for those who Love Time is
Eternity.

The Egyptians probably made the first sundials in around 2000 BC, using a simple crossbar whose shadow moved over a series of marks made on the ground. It was the Romans who perfected the sundial designs we know today – and took them into their private spaces, setting them in the centre of gardens featuring both colonnades and outdoor 'rooms' in order to catch the shadow of the sun god Sol as he crossed the sky each day.

By the Renaissance, there were sundials of every description, some recording dates and signs of the Zodiac. They were commonly placed in churchyards as symbolic reminders to the living that life is brief. A typical Latin inscription from around 1666 (the year of the great Fire of London) appears on a dial at Kirk Michael in the Isle of Man: *'Temporis memor mei, tibi posui monitorem.'* ('Mindful of my time, I have erected a warning for you.') When topiary came into fashion (see page 129) living sundials were sometimes made from clipped box or yew; an English example survives at Ascott House in Buckinghamshire.

The Sundial Trail in Ulster's County Down visits a selection of magnificent historic sundials. It begins in the Rose Garden in front of Bangor Town Hall, with an ancient vertical stone dial, originally erected around 900 AD in Bangor Monastery, of which nothing else now remains.

WATER IS THE LIFE AND SOUL OF A GARDEN

For both plants and, more especially, those who want to enjoy a garden to the full. Moving water calms and soothes the mind while gently stimulating the senses.

It is certain that water was an integral part of the earliest gardens. The Egyptians had ponds in their gardens where wildfowl could thrive. Water was also essential to the gardens of Islam, where it was intended to refresh and soothe the soul. Channels divided the garden into four – an idea that originated in early Persian gardens.

Water was also integrated into classical designs, such as the second-century Roman garden at Conimbriga in Portugal, where ponds and fountains were central to the layout, and the flowerbeds were constructed to look like floating islands. The Romans brought the fashion for fish ponds and fountains to Britain and built them on estates such as Fishbourne, near Chichester. In Renaissance gardens, passers-by were likely to be unexpectedly soaked by jets from trick fountains, or *giochi d'acqua*.

The radical 18th-century English landscape gardener, Lancelot 'Capability' Brown, replaced his clients' formal water gardens with natural-looking lakes and pools that blended into the landscape. The philosopher and statesman Francis Bacon (1561–1626), who expounded his forthright horticultural opinions in his essay *Of Gardens*, would not have approved – he was less enthusiastic about nature. 'For fountains,' he wrote, 'they are a great beauty and refreshment; but pools mar all, and make the garden unwholesome, and full of flies and frogs.' He also objected to the presence of fish. Today, a pond is as welcome in the garden for all the wildlife it attracts as for its aesthetics.

The magnificent 16th-century Organ Fountain at the Villa d'Este, near Tivoli in Italy, powers a water organ whose music inspired Franz Liszt when he stayed at the villa. It works on the ancient principles used by water engineers in second-century Alexandria.

WHO LOVES A GARDEN, LOVES A GREENHOUSE TOO

A line from a poem by William Cowper, in which he extols the pleasures of growing plants from warmer climes. Although a boon to the gardener, the greenhouse is not always the prettiest of garden structures.

The Romans cultivated plants kept warm in greenhouses 'glazed' with mica, but true glass was not used in Europe until the 15th century. By Elizabethan times, English gardeners were enjoying oranges and lemons cultivated in glasshouses heated by stoves developed in Holland. By the end of the 17th century the greenhouse was the equivalent of today's conservatory – not only a home for tender plants but a place of entertainment.

By the 18th century, the lean-to, often heated from beneath by hotbeds, had become a standard feature of the walled kitchen garden. Gertrude Jekyll held that an un-fancy, utilitarian design was best. 'The fatal thing,' she averred, 'is when an attempt is made to render the greenhouse ornamental, by the addition of fretted cast-iron ridges and fidgety finials.'

An unheated greenhouse is fine for raising cuttings and frost-tender seedlings of everything from basil to busy lizzies, and for crops of cucumbers and tomatoes, but warmth is a necessity for keeping tender plants over the winter. The greatest problem with the greenhouse is that it can get too hot in summer, killing plants and encouraging pests and diseases. Apart from opening greenhouse windows, whitening the glazing to reflect the light is an old-fashioned practice still highly recommended; for this job you need proprietary water-soluble white shading or lime wash, not ordinary whitewash. Alternatively, retractable blinds can be fitted.

One of the most famous glass houses ever built was the lily house at Chatsworth, designed for the Duke of Devonshire in the 1820s by Joseph Paxton, with ironwork based on the natural ribbing in the leaf of the giant Victoria water lily. Paxton went on to use the same principles in the construction of the Crystal Palace, erected in 1850–51.

LET THE WHEELBARROW DO THE WORK

Undoubtedly it is one of the world's greatest inventions. Gardeners through the centuries have been aware of the toll that their work can take on the health of their backs.

The wheelbarrow was certainly in use in China in the third century BC, though not in the garden but for carrying people and goods. It did not reach Europe until the Middle Ages. The design of the time was not the boxy device we know today – loads were set on a flat, long-handled barrow.

While moving quantities of earth during the building of Monticello, his mountaintop home in Virginia, US President Thomas Jefferson made an accurate comparison between the efficiency of single-wheeled and two-wheeled barrows. In a diary entry for 1772 he noted that: 'the two-wheeled barrow carries 4 loads of the single one at once … it will do exactly double the work in the same time, loading being equal.'

By the mid-19th century, wheelbarrows in a plethora of designs, both single- and two-wheeled, were available. Because at this time homes and greenhouses were heated with coal fires, cinders were sifted regularly and the ash made valuable fertilizer. The catalogue of the Manchester firm Follow & Bate included barrows fitted with cinder sifters on top. Other variations were wheelbarrows complete with 'shifting boards for carrying leaves, &c., fitted to barrow, for an extra 12 shillings above the price of £1.10 shillings.' (In pre-decimal currency there were 20 shillings to the pound.)

> During his stay in England in 1697, Tsar Peter the Great enjoyed being pushed about John Evelyn's garden at Sayes Court in Deptford in a wheelbarrow – at the cost of various plants, including a holly hedge, which were seriously damaged.

RAKE YOUR LEAVES

So that they don't look unsightly, and you can use them as compost and mulch. Some leaves are, however, best left where they fall.

Autumn leaves left on a lawn not only mar the general appearance of the garden but will make your grass turn a nasty yellow. In flowerbeds, however, they will not only retain warmth, and so help protect more delicate plants from frost – especially if you heap them up – but will gradually be pulled below the surface by worms, improving soil texture. As well as a leaf rake, an old-fashioned besom is good for sweeping leaves off small lawns, but if your garden is large a leaf blower (which pushes them into a pile) or sucker (which gathers them into a container) may be useful, as long as the leaves are dry.

GOOD FOR THE SOIL

If you have the space, consider making your own leaf mould which, when well rotted and dug into the soil, will encourage root growth and aid moisture retention. Traditionally this was done by digging a pit in a corner of the garden, into which leaves were swept or thrown, but a more practical solution is probably a 'cage' of netting or slatted wood. Whichever you choose, make sure that the leaves are turned regularly and kept damp, and be patient. It may take two years for one season's leaves to rot down completely. Avoid putting diseased leaves in your pile. Black spot and rust will spread through the heap and around the garden when the leaf mould is eventually used, even after several years.

The popular song Autumn Leaves *was adapted by Johnny Mercer from a French song of 1945,* Les Feuilles Mortes, *written by the French surrealist poet Jacques Prévert for Marcel Carné's 1946 film* Les Portes de la Nuit. *The music, by the Hungarian composer Joseph Kosma, had been written for a ballet,* Le Rendez-Vous, *created in 1945 by Roland Petit.*

CROCK YOUR POTS

Broken terracotta crocks
are the traditional choice
for improving drainage in pots,
but there are other things you
need to do to prevent pots getting
waterlogged. And no pot will drain
unless it has holes in the bottom.

Gravel or coarse sand also help drainage and, like crocks, should fill about one tenth of the space in the pot. Mixing potting compost with vermiculite (particularly good when weight is a consideration) or sharp sand, again about 10 per cent by volume, prevents waterlogging, too. A pot raised off the ground on bricks or special pot 'feet' will always drain better than one put straight on to the ground. Saucers are fine for unglazed terracotta pots, which, unlike plastic ones, dry out quickly through evaporation, but can easily retain too much water. In winter this can freeze and damage plant roots.

Prized plants have been grown in containers for centuries, and pots would have featured in the courtyards of Roman villas. Huge urns were the fashion in the French and Italian gardens of the 18th century.

Use polystyrene 'chips' from packing in place of crocks, or crumble pieces of polystyrene trays. Or save washed mussel shells to put in the bottoms of your pots.

Bill and Ben 'The Flowerpot Men' and their companion Little Weed made their British TV debut on Watch with Mother in 1952. Children (and adults) loved their nonsensical talk, rich in expressions like 'flobbadob' (flower pot) and 'bob bob' (goodbye).

Bring in the bees

Bees are not only a delight to see buzzing around the garden but are also important pollinators. Local beekeepers will thank you greatly for planting a bee-friendly garden.

As they visit flowers to delve for sugar-rich nectar, bees also gather the pollen that is an essential food for the hive. In doing so, they unwittingly carry pollen from bloom to bloom, thus ensuring that flowers are fertilized – a requisite for fruit formation in most species. Flowers and their pollinators evolved hand in hand, culminating in such extraordinary flower designs as the bee orchid, which looks like the insect it aims to attract.

Flowers are, remarkably, able to signal to bees that they are rich sources of pollen. Signals visible to us are, for instance, the spots on the lips of foxglove flowers and the yellow markings on the falls of irises. But bees see in the ultraviolet range of the spectrum, and other markings on the petals, which we cannot see, are clearly visible to guide bees to the nectar.

Planting for bees

There is plenty of choice when it comes to planting flowers that will be attractive to honeybees. A beekeeper would recommend an annual progression beginning with crocuses and snowdrops in early spring, through heathers, hebes, thymes and lavenders to the Michaelmas daisies of autumn. A hedge of flowering privet and ivy on walls will be magnets for bees.

In the vegetable garden, the broad bean has a remarkable association with bees, which use it in various distinct ways. Pollen and nectar are collected as honeybees enter the fronts of the flowers, but short-tongued bumble bees cut holes in the bases of the flowers to extract nectar. Honeybees then use these holes as entry points. In addition, honeybees are attracted to the black spots on the plant stipules. At the bases of these leaf-like structures are extra small pockets of nectar that is especially rich in sugar.

THE GARDENER WHO DOES NOT CARRY A NOTEBOOK MUST ALWAYS BE SURPASSED BY ONE WHO DOES

Though easier said than done, writing notes and drawing diagrams is the best way of recording what you have planted – and where. A camera is handy, too.

Labels, written in weatherproof ink, are other essential *aides memoires*, especially for bulbs, corms and tubers lifted for the winter, and for seeds and seedlings. For mature plants, the problem with most commercial labels is that they are unsightly. Good solutions are to make tags out of pieces of sawn wood, drilled and tied to plants, or to write or etch names on to stones placed below the plants.

The problem of labels is not new. Writing in 1901 about the 'Shakespeare Borders' in the garden of Lady Warwick, Alice Morse Earle remarks on '... the peculiar label set alongside each plant. This label is of pottery, greenish brown in tint, shaped like a butterfly, bearing on its wings a quotation of a few words and the play reference relating to each special plant. Of course these words have been fired in and are thus permanent. Pretty as they are in themselves they must be disfiguring to the borders – as all labels are in the garden.'

2. FABULOUS FLOWERS

Whatever the season, flowers are most surely the making of a garden. They bring colour and scent and, thanks to centuries of breeding, are available in almost every shade, scent and form imaginable. And although flowers look wonderful grown in pots and baskets, and it is possible to replant and redesign garden beds every year with a new selection of annuals, both the cottage garden and the old-fashioned herbaceous border remain hugely attractive and desirable.

Trends in gardening inevitably come and go, but there are some flowers that are always popular, including lilies, carnations, poppies and lupins. These, though now highly bred and available in a mass of varieties – many much hardier and disease resistant than their predecessors and in a wider range of colours – were the favourite of gardeners of old, and many have probably been cultivated for as long as gardens themselves.

As well as their blooms, many plants have beautiful foliage, which adds greatly to the magnificence of the garden; many flowers also mature into superb seed heads, which can last all through the winter. But it really does not matter what flowers you favour as long as you look after them with the loving care they deserve.

THE HUMBLE HELLEBORE MAKES FEW DEMANDS

Except that it prefers shade and a moist, moderately rich soil. Hellebores are especially welcome in the dark days of winter and early spring, when there are few other blooms to adorn the garden.

With good planning it is possible to have hellebores in bloom for months on end. First to flower is the Christmas rose *Helleborus niger*; the white-petalled flowers of the species may age to pink. Later in winter, coinciding with the pre-Easter fast whose name it shares, comes the Lenten rose (*H. orientalis*) whose colour range extends across purple and pink to white. Gertrude Jekyll rated hellebores as 'the most important flowers of their season, both for size and general aspect'. She especially recommended them for 'some place where wood and garden meet'.

Typified by its green flowers is the stinking hellebore (*H. foetidus*), which, as one might expect from its name, exudes an unpleasant, somewhat putrid smell. Unlike the green hellebore (*H. viridis*), it bears many flowers on each stem. Also green flowered is *H. argutifolius*, the Corsican hellebore.

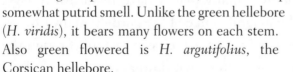

Hellebores have been used to treat illnesses in both animals and humans. The stinking hellebore was once used as a remedy for 'pestilence' in cattle, and to treat melancholia, epilepsy and paralysis in humans. The Christmas rose, however, was preferred as a cure for madness.

Do what you will, you will never lose a columbine

Especially if it is a single-flowered sort. Archetypal cottage garden plants, columbines are not only hardy but seed themselves freely and easily around flower beds.

John Parkinson, who wrote *Paradisi in Sole, Paradisus Terrestris* ('Park-in-Sun's Earthly Paradise') in 1629, perfectly summed up the attraction of these flowers: 'Columbines single and double, of many sorts, fashions and colours, very variable both speckled and partly coloured, are flowers of that respect, as that no Garden would willingly be without them … yet the rarer the flowers are, the more trouble to keep; the ordinary sorts on the contrary part will not be lost, do what one will.'

The columbine (*Aquilegia vulgaris*) is known in country places as 'granny's bonnet' from the shape of its spurred flowers. The rare wild flowers are plain purple, but in the garden, thanks to both natural and commercial hybridization, they come in a range of colours – from copper-orange and yellow to pale purple and white – and in both single and exuberant double forms. Though columbines rarely breed true, it is worth scattering the seeds from your favourite colours to see what you get.

> Some say the name Aquilegia comes from the Latin aqua, water, and lego, to collect, from the idea that water runs down the petals into the spurs. But a more likely suggestion is that the name is inspired by aquila, the Latin for eagle, because the flower's spurs resemble the bird's claws.

TAKE THE TOPS OUT OF HOLLYHOCKS

An old gardeners' trick for getting fine, pyramidal-shaped plants with plenty of side shoots, rather than a few giant spikes.

Left uncut, hollyhocks can easily reach more than 2.1m (7ft) in height. Although this 'topping', best done when the lower blooms are out, will temporarily spoil the appearance of the hollyhock, the result is the growth of many flower-bearing side shoots on the plant. If, however, you prefer your hollyhocks to grow as tall as possible – as when placed at the back of a border or at some other strategic position where they can break up ugly lines and 'explain their beauty to distant views' – then leave them to their own devices, although they may need staking in windy situations.

Though they are easy to grow from seed, young hollyhocks need avid protection from slugs and snails. Because they are prone to attack by rust (known as red rust or hollyhock disease), which seriously spoils the look of the leaves, any gardener seeking perfection will prefer to grow them as biennials.

A member of the mallow family, Malvacea, the hollyhock was originally classified, together with the marsh mallow, in the genus Althaea. It is now designated *Alcea rosea*.

ARCHITECTURAL MOTIF

While the hollyhock is a typical English cottage garden plant, it was also the inspiration for Hollyhock House in Los Angeles, which was built between 1919 and 1921 for oil heiress Aline Barnsdall by the architect Frank Lloyd Wright. The flower for which the building is named is rendered in abstract and geometric form in much of the house design, including exterior walls and interior furniture.

An infusion of dried hollyhock flowers is a traditional remedy for coughs and bronchitis. If used as a gargle it will also help to soothe mouth ulcers.

THROW WASHING-UP WATER ON LILIES

This old gardening adage reflects both the proverbial resilience of cottage garden lilies and their needs for constant moisture and protection against beetle attack. The white Madonna lily has long been a symbol of purity.

It is one of the ironies of gardening that some plants seem to thrive on healthy neglect. Lamenting her failure with Madonna lilies (*Lilium candidum*), the garden writer and illustrator Ethel Armitage observed that, in cottage gardens, 'The bulbs are torn from the ground at all seasons of the year, to be passed on to other cottage gardens, where they quickly settle down and become more beautiful than the polished corners of the Temple. And, as far as can be ascertained, no attention beyond the washing-up water, when it is quite finished with, is given them. And on this mixture of grease, strong soda and soap they are able to surpass Solomon in all his glory.'

Except for the Madonna lily, which should be planted in late summer, lily bulbs can be put into the ground at any time between mid-autumn and early spring. They like a soil enriched with compost or bonemeal and need good drainage. If the bulbs look rather dry, immerse them in damp potting compost for a few days to swell before you plant them.

Lilies can be extremely prone to attack by a number of pests and diseases. The moment the shoots emerge, they are magnets for slugs. Plants that are overcrowded and poorly nourished will be susceptible to botrytis mould. Bright red lily beetles and their larvae munch both leaves and flowers. Either remove the larvae from the plants by hand or wipe them off with a sponge soaked in soapy water.

Culpeper claimed that lilies were 'excellently good in pestilential fevers', recommending that patients drink a decoction made by boiling the roots in wine. For dropsy (a heart condition) his remedy was to mix juice from the plant with barley meal, which was then baked and eaten like ordinary bread. An ointment concocted by mixing the roasted root with a little hog's grease would, he said, 'cure burnings and scaldings without a scar, and trimly deck a blank place with hair'.

ANCIENT FLOWERS

The Madonna lily, depicted on Cretan vases of the Minoan period as early as 1650 BC, is one of the oldest flowers in cultivation. It was beloved of the Romans, who probably brought it to Britain. Pliny even experimented with making white flowers turn purple by steeping the bulbs in red wine. It was the Venerable Bede who, in the eighth century, wrote of the lily as the symbol of the Virgin Mary.

The headily scented regal lily (*L. regale*) was brought to the West from China by the plant hunter Ernest Henry Wilson. In 1910 he discovered it in a high valley but while gathering bulbs he was thrown down the mountain by a landslide and very nearly lost a leg. Luckily for us, he held on to the bulbs.

LILY STORIES, NAMES AND SYMBOLS

- *The lily sprang from the ground where Eve's tears fell when she was expelled from the Garden of Eden.*
- *The whiteness of the Madonna lily is a symbol of chastity.*
- *The angel Gabriel carries a white lily to symbolize his Annunciation to the Virgin Mary.*
- *The turk's cap or martagon lily is named from the shape that the recurved petals give to the flower.*
- *Smelling lilies is said to be a cause of freckles on the face.*
- *The tiger lily, with petals spotted in purple, is a symbol of passion.*

CULTIVATE HONESTY FOR ITS SEEDS

Or, technically, its flat, round, translucent seed heads, which are perfect for enhancing indoor flower arrangements. Honesty is an excellent plant for a semi-wild area of the garden, where it will seed itself freely.

As well as its seed heads, honesty earns its place in the garden for its purple or white flowers, borne in late spring and early summer. Select from *Lunaria annua* (syn. *biennis*), a biennial useful for the fact that it will tolerate dry shade, and *L. rediviva*, a short-lived perennial with showier flowers, which has more pointed seed heads. There is also a variegated cultivar of *L. annua* called 'Alba Variegata', whose leaves are prettily bordered with creamy white, a beautiful match for its white flowers.

To make sure the papery seed heads will keep well in dried arrangements, cut them in dry weather when they are fully ripe and store them in a dry place for a few days to harden up.

Other common names for this plant, all based on the shape of its seed heads, are moonwort (which is reflected in its scientific name *Lunaria*), money plant, satin flower, silver penny and silver dollar.

The proverb 'Honesty is the best policy' was first recorded in the 16th century.

> Writing in 1618 of the hired gardener's virtue (not the flower) the Yorkshire clergyman and horticulturalist William Lawson said: 'Honestie in a Gardener, will grace your Garden, and all your house ... hee will not purloin your profite, nor hinder your pleasures...'

Plant by the Rule of Three

An excellent piece of advice for setting plants and bulbs in borders and in containers. As well as groups of three, larger odd-numbered settings also work well.

Whether you are planting bulbs or bedding plants, groups of three will give you quantity without over-domination. Three or five plants also make a generous filling for a container, where two would look too sparse and four or six too many. And odd-numbered groups are far easier to arrange. Set a group of three plants in a triangular shape rather than in a line to concentrate their effect.

In medieval fields, crops were grown on a three-year cycle. In the first year wheat or rye was sown, and in the second peas, beans or barley. In the third year the land was allowed to rest or 'stand fallow'.

The Best Annuals for Shady Places are Biennials

One of the many maxims of Gertrude Jekyll, who designed more than 300 gardens. Her advice refers especially to foxgloves, mulleins and evening primroses.

All three of these plants do well in shade and will self-seed from year to year. Of all garden foxgloves, white ones such as *Digitalis albiflora* are among the most prized, but there are other unusual species, such as the pale orange rusty foxglove (*D. ferrugina*), the Grecian foxglove (*D. lanata*), with pale caramel flowers, and *D. ciliata*, which has small cream blooms. Of mulleins, Jekyll's favourites were the tall *Verbascum olympicum*, a native of Greece, and the quick-growing *V. phlomoides,* with larger, orange flowers. Today they come in a plethora of colours, including pink, lilac, white and russet. Beware, however, of the wild mullein (*V. thapsus*), which can be horribly invasive. And although it is very pretty when in flower, the common evening primrose (*Oenothera biennis*) seeds itself so freely that it, too, can be a nuisance.

COUNTRY WISE

In country places, wild versions of these garden flowers have many associations:

- *Because of its soft, woolly leaves, mullein is sometimes known as Adam's blanket or Adam's flannel. It is also called donkey's ears, hare's beard, Aaron's rod and Our Lady's candle.*
- *Mullein juice is an old remedy for a wide variety of complaints, from hoarseness to gout and piles.*
- *The roots of the evening primrose have a wine-like smell that is very attractive to wild animals.*
- *Foxgloves are believed to be the cloaks of fairies, though it is a related plant,* Erinus alpinus, *that is known as the fairy foxglove.*

Gertrude Jekyll (1843–1932) was one of the best-known garden designers of her time. She began her career as an artist, but failing eyesight led her to turn her attention to garden design.

Grow lupins for their celestial colour

A tribute to the blue lupin or lupine that grows wild in America and, in cultivated form, in temperate gardens all over the world. In the language of flowers the lupin is a symbol of caution against over-confidence.

Lupins are a must for the blue garden, though their slightly peppery scent is not to everyone's taste. If you have the space, cultivated lupins also look wonderful in large stands of mixed colours. But, although lovely in bloom, the plants quickly get tatty once the flowers fade and can be prone to attack by mildew. For this reason they are best cut down to ground level after flowering so that they can re-grow, or dug up and replaced with new plants the following year.

The first lupins to reach British gardens were the wild species from the Mediterranean, with flowers in white and shades of yellow or purple. The many colours we enjoy today are a tribute to the efforts of Yorkshireman George Russell, who used as his starting point *Lupinus polyphyllus*, collected in British Columbia by David Douglas in the 1820s. When the first Russell lupins went on sale in 1937 they caused a stir in gardening circles.

Lupin seeds have long been used by the Navajo to make a medicine that not only relieves boils but is a cure for sterility. It is even believed to be effective in producing girl babies.

Wild lupins

Drifts of the American wild blue lupin, or bluebonnet, are a wonderful sight. In his book *Summer*, Henry Thoreau, the 19th-century philosopher and naturalist, described how 'it paints a whole hillside with its blue … such a profusion of the heavenly, the Elysian colour…' He also extolled the way in which rain and dew settle in bright pools in the centres of lupin leaves.

DON'T BE TOO KIND TO NASTURTIUMS

Because they flourish in – and even prefer – poor soils. In rich ground they will make foliage in preference to the flowers which, as well as being delicious for humans are, like the leaves, a favourite food of caterpillars.

For quick colour, and to hide such unsightly items as compost heaps, rubbish bins, or even a bare bank, fast-growing garden nasturtiums (*Tropaeolum majus*) are an excellent choice. Seeds sown in mid-spring will, by midsummer, produce a profusion of foliage smothered in a colourful mass of flowers. As well as trailing types, look for small, bushy varieties of *T. minus*, which make pretty mounds in borders.

In old orchards, nasturtiums were once grown up trees to enhance the quality and quantity of fruit, and can well be used decoratively in such a way in the garden. They are also excellent for pots and hanging baskets, and make a splash when trained up a twiggy wigwam set into a large barrel or pot.

The original nasturtium, brought to Europe from the Andes in the 16th century, was the yellow-flowered *T. minus* or Indian cress, which became known as the 'Yellow Larkes Spurr'. John Gerard (who named it *T. indicum*) received it from his friend John Robin, keeper of the King's garden in Paris.

> The nasturtium's generic name comes from the Greek tropaion or 'trophy', because the flower and leaf resemble a helmet and shield, the traditional adornments of a warrior's monument.

PRETTY ENOUGH TO EAT

Nasturtium flowers make an unusual addition to a salad or a lively garnish. They have a peppery taste and contain a natural antibiotic. The pungent young leaves have long been eaten, and the name 'nasturtium', which means 'twisted nose' or 'nose stinger' (from the effects of the leaves) is Latin for cress.

Nasturtium seeds can be pickled and used like capers. Ripe seeds allowed to dry out thoroughly for a couple of days are sprinkled with salt then pickled in vinegar flavoured with garlic, shallots, allspice, cloves and mace.

For a quite different flavour, try growing the tuberous nasturtium (*T. tuberosum*). As well as red and gold flowers, it yields edible tubers that can be eaten raw or cooked like potatoes. A particular oddity of the tubers, a staple diet in parts of South America (where they are known as *mashua* or *ysaño*), is that their red stripes turn blue when they are cooked.

A NASTURTIUM FOR EVERY SETTING

Choose your variety by the use you have in mind; including these more unusual ones:

Trailers or climbers (varieties of T. majus)	'Climbing Mixed'	Cream, orange, yellow and cerise blooms
	'Alaska Mixed'	Fiery flowers and leaves that are mottled and marbled creamy white
Semi-trailers – ideal for hanging baskets (varieties of T. majus)	'Jewel of Africa'	Orange, red and yellow flowers, foliage splashed in white
	'Gleam' Series	Rich peachy-apricot, red and yellow flowers; bright green foliage
Bushy – for borders (varieties of T. minus)	'Tip Top Mahogany'	Mahogany-red flowers; golden-green foliage
	'Peach Melba'	Yellow flowers with orange markings

GROW AURICULAS IN A THEATRE

That is, on a series of staged shelves inside a painted wooden shelter, to protect the amazing flowers from the weather and show their superb colours to best effect.

In times past, auricula theatres might even have been painted with scenery to complete the effect. They ranged from wooden boxes hung on sheltered walls to large structures built into the walled gardens of grand country houses. The auriculas that command this level of protection and display are the so-called show or stage auriculas, varieties of *Primula auricula*, whose petals have a mealy coating, or farina, that is easily washed off by the rain. They come in a fabulous array of colours, from deep purple and cream to black and white, with contrasting centres, edges and stripes.

Sacheverell Sitwell described the show auricula most evocatively in 1948: 'It is hardly to be conceived possible that such a plant should exist at all. There is something unreal and improbable in its edging and mealing. This latter has been stippled or dappled on to it. The white, mealy eye of the flower is a glorious and wonderful thing; but the slight and miraculous powdering on the back of the flower is even more striking … And the perfect corona of so many heads in flower, the cluster, or truss, has the plenitude, the richness, of a Bacchic bunch of grapes.'

Border auriculas, which may or may not have farina on their leaves and flowers, are less fussy and will thrive in a moist bed. They demand partial shade and well-drained soil. Being native to the Alps and Dolomites, they love chalk.

The common name for the auricula is the mountain cowslip. Probably brought to Britain by the Huguenots before 1700, it quickly became a florists' favourite.

GRADE A BORDER BY HEIGHT

The commonsense way to plan herbaceous borders, though not a rule to adhere to with absolute rigidity. Within this plan, simplicity is one of the keys to success.

As well as putting tall plants at the back of the border and shorter ones at the front, it's best to group plants rather than scattering them around the border. Remember, too, that plants with relatively low-growing foliage, such as foxgloves and delphiniums, send up tall flower spikes.

Our modern style of herbaceous border owes much to the Irish-born Victorian gardener William Robinson, who worked in England from 1861, initially at Regent's Park. Much influenced by the Arts and Crafts movement, he favoured a natural style of gardening in place of the complex, ultra-formal looks then in fashion. He put his ideas into practice at Gravetye Manor in West Sussex.

ROBINSON'S RULES

Some key points from the expert that still hold good today, taken from The English Flower Garden, 1896 edition:

- *Select only good plants; throw away any weedy kinds.*
- *Let each good thing be so bold and so well grown as to make its presence felt.*
- *Do not [always] graduate the plants in height from front to back … sometimes let a bold plant come to the edge.*
- *Plant in naturally disposed groups.*
- *Have no patience with bare ground … let little ground plants form broad patches and colonies … let them pass into and under other plants.*
- *Do not pay too much attention to labelling. If a plant is not worth knowing, it is not worth growing.*

When planting a border from scratch, or making major renovations, make a plan on squared paper, noting colour and flowering seasons as well as height and spread. Leave space for plants to grow and mature – you can plant bulbs and bedding plants as temporary space fillers.

SAXIFRAGES SIT HAPPILY BETWEEN STONES

A tribute to the tolerance of these plants, which are the mainstays of the rock garden, but also useful in all kinds of situations where conditions are tough.

When choosing a saxifrage for the rock garden or to plant in gravel it is helpful to be aware of the main groups into which the experts divide them. Silver saxifrages, whose grey-green leaves are encrusted with beads of lime, will, understandably, do best in limey soil. Tolerant of both drought and shade, they will reward you with showers of flowers, usually white, in late spring and early summer.

Cushion saxifrages are small, slow-growing, winter-flowering plants and, as long as they are not exposed to hot sun, will grace the rock garden. The flowers come in reds, yellows and purples. Mossy saxifrages, as their name suggests, make soft cushions of foliage, topped with long-stemmed flowers, in late spring and early summer. A saxifrage that will grow almost anywhere is *Saxifraga umbrosa* or London Pride. It is also easily propagated: pieces taken off the parent plant will root at almost any time of year.

Because it grows in cracks in rocks the saxifrage is commonly known as 'breakstone'. Medicinally, it was thought to be able to break up kidney stones. In Britain it was chewed to dispel toothache and fade freckles, while in Italy eating the root was said to increase a girl's beauty.

PLANT CROCUSES IN DRIFTS

A good planting tip for getting the best effects and to help disguise any damage resulting from attack by birds. If you can plant lavender nearby, this may also help to deter birds from pecking your crocuses to pieces.

The best places for drifts of crocuses – and a pageant of colour – are sunny banks, around shrubs and under trees. Though they will not make drifts, groups of crocuses in a rockery can also be extremely effective. For the best display, keep different varieties distinct, planting corms about 7.5cm (3in) deep and the same distance apart. In a lawn, make small V-shapes in the grass with a spade, peel back the turf and pop the corms into the soil before replacing the sward.

Crocuses are probably attractive to birds because of the vitamin and energy-rich pollen in their brightly coloured centres; sparrows will also peck away at primroses when they come into flower. Varieties that flower later, when there is more food around, are less prone to attack. There are dozens of shades of yellow, white and purple to choose from, with reproductive organs in yellow, orange or deep red. As to cultivation, the Scottish gardener James Justice (1698–1763) strongly advised using a dibble (dibber) for making planting holes, and adding a little soot to each hole to prevent attacks from mice.

You can see spring crocuses growing wild in the mountains of Turkey, Spain and Portugal. All the modern purple and white crocuses, however, are derived from *C. vernus*, which is a native of Italy, Austria and Eastern Europe.

PRECIOUS SPICE AND DYE

The anthers of the purple-flowered autumn crocus *Crocus sativus* are the source of saffron, used in cooking for its colour and its spicy, bitter flavour, and as a dye. The Moghuls are thought to have introduced it to India and Persia before the third century BC. Though introduced to Britain by the Romans, its cultivation died out until, in the 14th century, a pilgrim returning from the Holy Land is purported to have smuggled home a single precious corm in his staff – which he had hollowed out for the purpose.

It takes up to 4,500 flowers to make just 28g (1oz) of saffron. The stigmas are still picked laboriously by hand. Don't confuse this crocus with meadow saffron (*Colchicum autumnale*), which grows wild in Britain. This crocus is poisonous in all its parts; it contains the toxic substance colchicine, which has been used as a remedy for gout since ancient times.

EXTENDING THE SEASON

Stagger the flowering season with a range of varieties, including autumn crocuses:

Mid-winter	C. imperati (dark and pale violet), C. laevigatus 'Fontenayi' (lilac, outer petals striped deep purple)
Late winter	C. vernus 'Remembrance (dark violet), C. chrysanthus 'Advance' (yellow), C. minimus (pale biscuit coloured outer petals with purple veins, bright purple inner petals)
Early spring	C. sieberi 'Albus' (white), C. tommasinianus (pale lilac inner petals, silvery purple outer petals), C. vernus cultivars including 'Jeanne d'Arc' (pure white petals with deep purple bases)
Early autumn	C. banaticus (lilac)
Mid-autumn	C. boryi (white, purple veins), C. goulimyi (pale lilac)
Late autumn	C. cartwrightianus (lilac, red stigmas), C. ochroleuchus (pale cream flowers with yellow throats)

CHOOSE GROUND COVER FOR ITS FOLIAGE

And also its flowers, though it is the good-looking leaves that should be your primary consideration when choosing ground cover plants. You need plants that, without being too invasive or swamping other specimens, will quickly cover the exposed soil in your beds and borders.

> Carrying periwinkle is an old protection against evil and is said to bring prosperity. In Italy it is planted on the graves of children to protect their souls. Periwinkle is also an old cure against possession by the Devil, but for use as a cure, ancient herbals recommend that it should be picked only on the 'first, ninth, eleventh or thirteenth nights of the moon'.

Ideally ground cover should look good all year round, which makes variegated evergreens such as the small-leaved ivy *Hedera* 'Spetchley' a good choice, though many gardeners hate ivy anywhere in their gardens, most of all in flower beds. The same goes for miniature bamboos such as *Pleioblastus viridistriatus,* which, like other bamboos, can not only run riot if left unchecked but can look tatty after a few years.

Good old-fashioned flowering ground cover plants include the common bugle, *Ajuga reptans*, now bred in varieties with spectacular foliage, among them 'Atropurpurea', whose purple leaves are tinted with bronze, and 'Burgundy Glow', which has whitish green leaves splashed with red.

The periwinkle is another old favourite, useful because, as long as it is not allowed to dry out completely, it will happily tolerate shade. Of the species commonly available *Vinca major* is, as its name suggests, larger leaved than *V. minor*. Both come in plain and variegated forms, and with flowers in the white-mauve range.

NEVER MOVE A PEONY

A peony will last a lifetime as long as you resist the temptation to move it from one bed to another. Peony tubers are prized in legend for their healing powers, and it is said that uprooting one will bring the worst of ill fortune.

Named after the Greek physician Paeon, peonies (*Paeonia* spp) have been cultivated since at least the seventh century, when the Chinese grew them for their medicinal properties and their beauty. Today's gardener can choose from a huge range of species and varieties, from the sumptuous, ruffled double pink *P. lactiflora* 'Sarah Bernhardt' to *P. mlokosewitchii*, known colloquially as 'Molly the Witch', whose soft bluish-green foliage is topped with single lemon yellow flowers.

Peonies need a fertile, well-composted soil and plenty of sunshine, though they are prone to damage by spring frosts if iced leaves are warmed quickly by bright sunshine. They arrived in Britain in profusion in the 1880s and their cultivation reached the height of fashion in Edwardian times. Favourites of the period were the large, often double-flowered, cultivars of *Paeonia lactiflora* imported from China and grown in preference to the 'ordinary' red single-flowered European native, *P. officinalis*.

QUEEN OF FLOWERS

The moutan or tree peony (*P. suffruticosa*), a native of Western China, is a large shrub, not a herbaceous perennial. It was introduced to Japan by Buddhist missionaries in the eighth century, and has given rise to many hybrids, with finely cut foliage and showy, double flowers in colours from white and pale apricot to deep carmine. They are distinguished, long-lived shrubs, requiring rich, well-drained soil.

> John Parkinson, writing in 1640 on cures for epilepsy said: 'I saw a child freed from that disease, that had for eight whole months together, worn a good piece of the [peony] root about him.'

CARNATIONS ARE CREATURES OF TEMPERAMENT

While some carnations will grow with ease, others are fussy, and most will die after about three years. It is said that beds for these plants, like beds in the best-kept houses, should always be well aired and well made.

There are dozens of different carnations to choose from, but the most reliable are the border carnations and garden pinks – to raise the perpetual-flowering varieties you really need a greenhouse. Bred from *Dianthus caryophyllus*, border carnations are hardy perennials with grey or blue-grey leaves. Garden pinks, which have a heady scent, have been bred from a variety of species.

To avoid stem rot, plant dianthus with the lowest leaves well above soil level. To encourage side shoots, pinch out the tops in spring. If, however, you want to produce large, single flowers, then as well as taking out the main shoot when the plant has about ten pairs of leaves (to leave six pairs) any flower buds that grow below the main shoot should also be removed.

FOOLPROOF LAYERING

To ensure vigorous, healthy carnations, use one- or two-year-old plants for layering. In midsummer, after flowering, take a budless side shoot and bend it over so that it touches the soil. Remove all but the top three or four pairs of leaves and make a slit in the exposed stem, then press this part into the soil, holding it in place with a bent piece of wire. If you keep it well watered (but not waterlogged) roots should sprout in about six weeks. It can then be cut off and replanted.

- *The carnation, or clove-pink, was once known as the gilliflower. Like the second part of its scientific name,* caryophyllus, *the word comes from the Greek for 'nut leaved' – because its flowers have a scent like that of the clove tree (*Eugenia caryophylla*).*
- *Pinks were not named for their colour (which may in fact have been named after them), but possibly from the Dutch* pink-ogg, *meaning a small eye that twinkles or winks.*
- *Even in medieval times there were hundreds of carnation varieties, with exotic names such as red and blue halo and striped savage.*
- *The sweet william (*Dianthus barbatus*) probably got its common name in honour of William, Duke of Cumberland, who defeated Bonnie Prince Charlie at the Battle of Culloden in 1746.*
- Dianthus *varieties are classified in five colourways and distinctive shapes:* self *(single, uniform colour);* bicolour *(central eye in a contrasting colour);* laced *(contrasting colour at each petal edge and in a central blotch);* fancy *(contrasting but irregular markings); and* picotee *(contrasting colour at each petal edge).*

VIOLETS LIKE SUN WHILE FLOWERING

But shade for the rest of the year. Because they need clean air to thrive, violets were once prized by townsfolk and sold in the streets by the likes of the fictional Eliza Doolittle.

The sweet violet, *Viola odorata*, is a superb and longstanding addition to the scented garden. When growing wild, the violet favours banks where, once flowering is over, the surrounding vegetation will grow tall enough to shade its leaves, and it appreciates a similar environment in the garden, whether naturalized in grass or used to edge herbaceous borders.

Despite their name, species violets are not always purple. The pretty wood violet (*V. biflora*) is yellow, while the hairy violet (*V. hirta*) may be white. A distinctive reddish tinge typifies the flowers of the prairie violet (*V. pedatifida*). Heartsease, the wild pansy (*V. tricolor*), is, as its name suggests, a mixture of purple, yellow and white.

During his exile on Elba in 1814, Napoleon's followers nicknamed him Corporal Violette, 'the little flower that returns in spring', and adopted the flower as their badge. Coloured prints of a bouquet of violets circulated among Bonapartists, containing hidden portraits of Napoleon, his wife Marie Louise and their son. As a result, any portrayal of a violet was officially banned in France, and the veto remained in force until 1874.

CLASSICAL VIOLETS

The Greeks used violets to make garlands for festivals while the Romans candied the petals and also used the flowers to make violet wine.

In Greek legend the flower is said to have sprung from the blood of Ajax, a hero of the Trojan War, after he killed himself following a dispute with Odysseus. An alternative story is that when he was discovered dallying with the priestess Io by his wife Hera, Zeus turned Io into a white heifer and created violets to be her special food.

In the Victorian language of flowers the 'pure and sweet' violet is the bloom of modesty. When white it symbolizes innocence, while the blue flower signifies faithful love.

Irises are nature's sun lovers

A truth that immediately determines their ideal position in the garden. The earliest mentions of irises in cultivation stress their healing properties, notably those of the 'roots', which we now know to be rhizomes.

Bearded irises (so called from the prominent hairs on their three lower petals, or falls) come in almost every colour and size, from the miniature apricot *Iris attica* to the tall white *I. pallida* 'Snowy Owl'. Leaving the top of each rhizome exposed to the sun is vital to ensure flowering. A good tip is to set rhizomes with their leaves to the north, preventing them from casting a shadow over the rhizome.

Beardless irises also grow from rhizomes, but these prefer to be buried under the soil rather than being exposed. In these irises the tops of the falls are often splashed with yellow or another sharply contrasting colour to attract insect pollinators.

Bulbous irises, such as the small spring-flowering purple *I. reticulata* and yellow *I. danfordiae*, also relish sunny locations and look best planted in showy clumps, though even if well tended, and fed regularly after flowering and until their foliage fades, they do not always last more than a year after planting. It may help to dig up the bulbs and store them over the winter.

Curative powers

'All iris roots,' said the Greek herbalist Dioscorides, 'have a warm, soothing facility, excellent for use in coughs. They purge thick humours and choler … Drunk with vinegar they help such as are bitten by venomous beasts, those suffering from the spleen, those troubled with convulsions, such as are chilled and stiff with cold, and such as let fall their food.'

The wild iris is commonly called a flag, from the Middle English flagge, meaning a sword – a reference to the shape of the leaves. The three falls are believed to symbolize courage, faith and wisdom.

Don't cut the green tops off your daffodils ...

... or other bulbs. They rely on their leaves to continue photosynthesizing well after the flowers have faded. To boost the bulbs' resources even more, and to keep plants looking neat, regular deadheading is highly recommended.

For the gardener who loves total tidiness, the problem with daffodils is that the leaves not only get to look very messy but carry on being green well into summer. For this reason, a good alternative to planting daffodils in borders is to naturalize them under trees or on areas of the lawn that can happily be left unmown until the leaves have faded. Alternatively there may be a spare corner – perhaps in the vegetable plot – to which they can be moved before being dug up, dried off, labelled and planted again in autumn.

Another way to avoid great masses of daffodil leaves is to choose miniature varieties such as the unusual hoop petticoat daffodil (*Narcissus bulbocodium*) with wide yellow trumpets and *N. jonquilla* with its groups of up to four tiny but highly fragrant flowers.

Also called the Lent Lily, the daffodil is the national flower of Wales and is worn on 1 March, St David's Day. Children used to gather wild daffodils for sale, as A.E. Houseman recounted in The Shropshire Lad:

The boys are up the woods with day,
To fetch the daffodils away,
And home at noonday from the hills
They bring no dearth of daffodils.

> Whoever finds
> the first daffodil
> in spring will, it
> is said, be blessed
> with more gold
> than silver.

In time, daffodils become overcrowded and begin to flower less profusely, or even become blind, so it is worth digging up clumps every few years to separate the bulbs and replant them. This is best done when the foliage has turned yellow. If they fail to do well after such division, dig them out and start again with fresh stock.

DAFFODIL HYBRIDS

In early horticultural texts, the true daffodil was deemed to be the white poet's narcissus. The yellow trumpet-flowered kind was long considered unworthy of the name and was dubbed 'pseudo-narcissus'. However, both became popular in England, with new species added to gardeners' collections by travellers and merchants who bought bulbs from as far away as Constantinople. By 1630 the English apothecary and gardener John Parkinson had acquired no fewer than 78 different types.

Although they grow so readily from bulbs, it is by growing daffodils from seed and crossing one species with another that new types are produced. This practice was established by the 17th century but took off in earnest after 1837, when Dean Herbert of Manchester published the results of his breeding experiments. There are now thousands of named varieties.

BULB DEPTH EQUALS TWICE BULB HEIGHT

A handy guide for planting most kinds of bulbs – though there are some notable exceptions to this rule.

Bulbs set too near the surface are unlikely to flower well. The hints for planting set out by Francis Hadfield Farthing in his 1920s gardening classic *Every Day in My Garden* still hold good today: 'Plant all kinds of bulbs with care and deliberation. It is not enough to thrust them anyhow into soil … Casual planting in heavy soil may result in the bulb being thrust out of the ground as soon as root action becomes vigorous.' He recommends a trowel over a dibber, warning that the latter 'tends to harden the walls of the cavity and prevent rapid root formation'.

Bulbs that need deeper than normal planting include lilies that have roots on their stems. These need setting three or four times deeper than their height. Madonna lily bulbs, on the other hand, like to have their tips just breaking the surface.

In flower beds bulbs also need room to spread, but different rules apply when planting them in containers. In this case they can be put very close together – or even touching – and in a deep pot they can be planted in more than one layer so as to produce maximum impact when they flower.

PENSTEMONS FLOWER BEST WHEN YOUNG

It is well worth taking cuttings from your favourite varieties of these long-flowering perennials, or raising new plants from seed each year. From the shape of their tubular flowers, penstemons are also known as beardtongues.

The Victorian gardener William Robinson summed up the usefulness of penstemons to perfection: 'Varied in colour, profuse in flower and of graceful habit,' he wrote in *The English Flower Garden*, 'Penstemons have a value for our flower-beds and rock-gardens that few other plants possess, especially as their blooming season extends five months commencing in June ...' Judicious choice of species will undoubtedly provide continuous colour, from the early rose pinks of the alpine *Penstemon newberryi* to the later cultivars such as 'Papal Purple'.

The Anglo-American botanist John Mitchell was the first person to write a scientific description of the penstemon in 1748. The plant's name derives from the flower's five stamens. In 1753 Linnaeus included it in his plant list, under the name *Chelone penstemon*.

> Penstemon root is an old North American cure for toothache.

OVERWINTERING

Though penstemons will last over the winter, what they hate most is a combination of frost and wet – conditions diametrically opposite to those in California, the home of 58 native species. And you should wait until winter is over to cut down the previous year's growth – it will serve as protection from frost.

POPPY SEEDS LIE LONG DORMANT

A fact borne out by the poppies that sprang up in Flanders' fields during World War I when the ground was massively disturbed. Ever since, and because of its blood red petals, the poppy has been associated with remembrance of the victims of war.

Science bears out the facts of poppy seed dormancy, though it also proves that after 50 years only some 5 per cent of seeds actually remain viable. But given that just one poppy plant can produce up to 500,000 seeds, this is still plenty. Like most other seeds, poppy seeds need a period of rest – ideally in the dark and cold – before they will germinate and start to grow into new plants. In temperate regions this is a survival mechanism, which ensures that new plants sprout into life only when growing conditions are favourable.

Garden poppies (*Papaver* spp) are summer's jewels, and were perfectly described by John Ruskin, the influential 19th-century art critic: 'The Poppy is the most transparent and delicate of all the blossoms … The rest, nearly all of them, depend on the texture of their surface for colour. But the Poppy is painted glass; it never glows as brightly as when the sun shines through it … it is a flame, and warms the wind like a blown ruby … When the flower opens, it seems a deliverance from torture.'

Poppy species to choose for the garden range from the annual or short-lived evergreen perennial Iceland poppy (*P. nudicaule*), whose bright yellow, orange or red flowers have a sweet scent, to the many varieties of the perennial oriental poppy (*P. orientale*), ranging from the rich salmon pink 'Mrs Perry' to the deep red 'Curlilocks', whose petals are deeply fringed. For an annual splash of colour there are few flowers to beat the scarlet of the common poppy (*P. rhoeas*).

THE POPPY OF SLEEP

Of all the poppies in cultivation in the West, the one with the longest history is the opium poppy, aptly named *P. somniferum*. Classical mythology relates that the plant was created by Somnus, the god of sleep, to ease the plight of the grain goddess Ceres, when she was wakeful with anxiety while searching for her lost daughter Proserpine, who had been carried off to the underworld. The flower sprang up in her path and, refreshed by sleep, she was once more able to tend the harvest, which she had neglected, and save humankind from starvation.

Many modern varieties of this annual have extravagantly double flowers in shades of pink, red, purple or white. The narcotic opium is made from the sap contained within the unripe seed heads.

SAVE SEED HEADS

And you will have plants for another year. If they are attractive, leave them on the plants to beautify the autumn garden – they also make wonderful additions to indoor arrangements.

While many perennials benefit from deadheading, there are others whose seed heads are almost as good-looking as their flowers. Most striking of all are those with distinctive shapes, such as poppy, love-in-a-mist, teasel and honesty (see page 41). *Echinops* also makes a good display.

Grasses such as *Pennisetum*, *Hordeum* and *Miscanthus* have long-lasting heads that look magnificent when sparkling with dew or winter frost – as do the fluffy heads of clematis. It is easy to see why the wild clematis is dubbed 'old man's beard' by country folk.

If you want to save your own seeds to raise plants for the following year, remember that those of F1 hybrids will not come 'true' – though this may not stop you experimenting. A good technique is to tie a paper bag over a seed head that is coming to maturity. When the seeds are ripe, shake them so that they fall into the bag and snip off the head from its stalk.

USE SMALL POTS FOR MORE FLOWERS

Particularly if you are growing pelargoniums, which are often (wrongly) dubbed geraniums. A pot that is too big will encourage leaves rather than flowers.

Putting pot plants under stress by packing them tightly encourages them to flower. Because they 'feel' threatened, their physiology induces them to reproduce as quickly as possible. A mature pelargonium needs a pot no bigger than 13cm (5in). Frequent deadheading and avoidance of overwatering help to ensure a profusion of flowers all summer long. Water pelargoniums only when the soil is dry. Test it with your fingers or tap the pot if it is terracotta – it will emit a ringing sound when the soil inside is dry.

Though they belong to the same family, pelargoniums are botanically distinct from the true geraniums, or cranesbills, which include many excellent hardy border perennials. Of the different sorts of pelargonium grown in the garden it is the so-called zonal types, with distinctive horseshoe markings on their leaves, that are most often called 'geraniums'. Other valuable types are the trailing ivy-leaved pelargoniums, which like to be packed into hanging baskets, and regal pelargoniums with their all-green, serrated leaves.

> *Housewives' tip: it's said that keeping a pelargonium on the windowsill will keep flies out of the house. Snakes are believed to be scared away by their peppery scent.*

FEED GENTIANS ON THE BLOOD OF KINGS

An old saying that reflects the pride of place these beauties deserve, and their regal associations. They are fussy, and are reputed to break both the hearts and pockets of gardeners.

Pure air and sunlight, plus well-drained soil – an imitation of their alpine niche – is what gentians need. They must have soil that is neutral or, even better, rich in lime. However, the willow gentian (*Gentiana asclepiadea*) and other autumn-flowering types demand woodland conditions: plenty of leaf mould, moisture and partial shade.

It is the colour of their blooms that makes gentians such a joy. While some are white, yellow or red, it is the blue ones, such as the trumpet gentian (*G. acaulis*), that really command attention. Close planting, and mingling with the roots of other plants, suits gentians, again mimicking growing conditions in their mountain habitat.

HEALING POWERS

Gentians are named for Gentius, King of Illyria in the second century BC, who was the first person to use the plant medicinally. Another legend relates that, in his search for a cure for the plague, the Hungarian King Ladislaus shot an arrow into the air, which he prayed would produce a remedy. It landed in a gentian plant. Mixed with wine, gentian root is a herbal treatment prescribed for aching joints. In the Alps the same mixture is recommended for relieving travel fatigue.

'CHIT' SWEET PEA SEEDS TO MAKE THEM GERMINATE

Nicking or chitting the hard outer covering of sweet pea seeds with a sharp knife helps water penetrate and thus speeds germination, but this treatment is best applied only if the seeds have failed to swell up after soaking in cold water overnight.

Another reliable method is to spread the seeds on dampened paper towels until they germinate, then plant them out. Sweet pea growers aiming for show success plant seeds of *Lathyrus odoratus* in mid-autumn and keep them over the winter in a cold frame, though for most gardeners early spring sowings will give a good long show of blooms. Sweet peas sown on St Patrick's Day, 17 March, are said by some to produce the largest blooms. For a wonderful scent, the best varieties to choose are the old-fashioned ones, such as 'Painted Lady' or 'Royal Wedding', or mixtures with names such as 'Antique Fantasy'.

Sweet peas, native to Sicily, were first cultivated in Britain in the 17th century. A wigwam of willow sticks makes an attractive support, but avoid ash: it is said to make the climber's tendrils recoil from its touch.

PUT USED TEA BAGS IN THE BOTTOM OF HANGING BASKETS

This modern-day tip aids water retention a little, though it is no substitute for regular soakings. Water-retaining granules are also helpful, especially when mixed with good compost.

However you plant up your baskets, and even with moisture-retentive liners such as foam or cardboard, most need a good watering almost every day, especially if they are in a sheltered position where they are unlikely to get rained on. If the basket is high up you will need a ladder, or a long-handled watering can or pump – more practical than dipping baskets in soft water twice a day in hot weather, as was once recommended.

Choosing drought-tolerant plants is another good way to prevent hanging baskets becoming too much of a chore to maintain. As well as pelargoniums (see p 64), begonias, verbenas, buzy lizzies, petunias, nasturtiums and brachysomes (Swan River daisies) will all cope with some drying out. Low-maintenance ivy makes a great leafy foil for basket flowers, from winter pansies and spring primulas to summer fuchsias. Don't forget to feed your hanging basket plants as well as watering them. Slow release granules are a great help and often come ready mixed with gel.

Hanging baskets are not new: the mosaics of a Roman villa found at Brading on the Isle of Wight depict hanging baskets of flowers – and peacocks.

A CIRCLE OF TWIGS IS A BETTER SUPPORT THAN A SINGLE STAKE

Good advice for protecting perennials, especially, and a way of creating a natural look in the garden. Staking early, though often easier said than done, is another top tip for the border.

For plants that tend to flop over or are exposed to wind, supports made from thin, twiggy branches are ideal to stop them breaking off and being marred by the weather, and can be cut to a height appropriate to each plant. If you wish, the twigs can be interlaced with raffia or soft green string. An alternative is to use a circle of bamboo canes. But be careful how you tie in tender shoots. Using strips cut from old tights can help to avoid damage and the ties are relatively inconspicuous.

KEEP IT NATURAL

When tying in, you also need to take into consideration the natural shape of the plant. As John Coutts of Kew advised in *All About Gardening* in 1931: 'Stems should be so tied that they maintain their natural distances apart; if bunched tightly together they will be deprived of a large amount of sun and air and will suffer heavily as a consequence … They should be able to sway naturally with the wind, if they cannot the blooms will offer resistance and may be torn or damaged.'

DIVIDE PERENNIALS IN AUTUMN

Autumn is probably the best time for increasing your stock of plants, and for reinvigorating any perennials that have become large and overgrown, but it is by no means a hard and fast rule.

The best time to divide perennials depends on the weather. If the early autumn is warm, autumn division will give plants time to re-establish themselves before frosts set in. Warmth is essential for some plants, including kniphofias, asters and delphiniums, and these are definitely best left until spring. Waiting until spring is also advisable if your soil is heavy and damp.

When dividing a perennial, dig it up first – don't try taking pieces from around the sides of the plant. Split a large plant using two border forks set back to back or, if you can, pull the clump apart with your hands. If all else fails you may need to slice it up with a spade. Discard the woody centre and any pieces with weak-looking roots and be sure to compost the soil well before you replant. Water well.

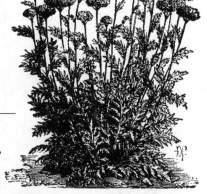

Divide and save: perennials bought from nurseries can often be divided before planting, giving you extra plants for your money.

Take time to appreciate the autumn garden. As Alfred Austin, the famous rose grower, wrote in 1894: 'Autumn adds such wonderful touches of happy accident that, when it comes, really comes, a wise man leaves his garden alone and allows it to fade, and wane, and slowly, pathetically, pass away, without any effort to hinder or conceal its decay. Indeed, it would be worthwhile having a cultivated garden if only to see what Autumn does with it.'

3. BETTER FRUIT AND TASTY VEGETABLES

HOCHSTEIN DEL.

However small your plot, growing your own fruit and vegetables is one of the great delights of gardening. Whether you have a whole garden full of crops, or just a few fruit trees and some tomatoes growing in pots, there are few tastes that can better that of home-grown produce eaten just a few minutes after picking.

Although the growers of prize-winning leeks, marrows and the like are loath to reveal their secrets, many of the memorable 'wise words' for gardeners relate to the vegetable garden or allotment. That may be because many of the best ways of preparing the ground for fruit and vegetables, and the timetable of sowing, planting and general care, go back to the old ways of farming. Notable among these are the need for composting and the practice of rotating crops to stop the soil becoming 'stale' and to prevent diseases lingering. For keeping crops fed, and improving the texture and water retention of the soil, there is still nothing to beat the application of good, well-rotted farmyard manure.

As in the flower garden, new varieties, especially those bred to resist diseases such as root fly and club root, are a boon to the modern gardener, but some old tips – such as pinching the tops out of broad beans to prevent black fly – still hold good today.

You need straw for strawberries

To keep the fruit off the earth and help prevent them getting dirty, rotten and prey to slugs and snails. Strawberries, eaten with cream, are the epitome of summer, inextricably linked with lawn tennis at Wimbledon.

'Strawing' strawberries must be done with a light and careful touch because, from the time the first blossoms appear to the full ripening of the fruit, the ground must never be allowed to dry out. To keep moisture in, a mulch is ideal. Bark chippings will work adequately, but well-rotted manure, with a thin layer of straw over it, is of more benefit to the plants. When rainwater is scarce, water each plant directly at its base. 'Tickling' the leaves with spray is virtually useless.

Small, sharp-flavoured strawberries have almost certainly been picked from the hedgerows since humans started gathering wild food. Strawberry plants have been cultivated since the 13th century, but the large juicy fruit we eat today did not appear until after 1819, when gardeners crossed the scarlet Virginian strawberry (*Fragaria virginiana*) with the pale Chilean strawberry (*F. chiloensis*).

Medical connections: A strawberry mark is the name for a raised red birthmark. Strawberry juice has long been applied to the skin to whiten it and fade freckles, and to the teeth to remove tartar.

THIN OUT APPLES AND PEARS

And peaches, too, if you have them, providing you have a heavy
'set' of fruit. As with seedlings, thinning the small fruit is the
best way to get better, bigger crops from your orchard trees.

Fruit needs thinning because, on a healthy tree, far more small fruits are produced than will ever be able to mature. Some will drop naturally, but the remainder need to be thinned carefully by hand, to about 15cm (6in) apart, though on a large, mature apple or pear tree this may be practically impossible. Remove blemished and central or 'king' fruits from the clusters first.

If, even after thinning, your branches are heavily laden, prop them up with V-shaped sticks while the fruits are still small. This will help to prevent the branches from breaking as the fruit matures.

INSECT ATTACK

Unwanted thinning of an apple crop happens when fruits are attacked by sawfly larvae – creamy white maggots that devour the hearts of the young fruits. The favoured treatment, ideally carried out a week after petal fall, is to spray with a product based on bifenthrin or pyrethrin. If you have the space and inclination, let chickens feed in your orchard. They are brilliant at eating sawfly larvae as they hatch out of cocoons in the soil.

Your apples and pears may also be under attack from the codling moth, whose caterpillars turn the cores brown and rotten. To help reduce attacks, buy a pheromone moth trap. This open-sided box is hung in the tree in late spring; in its base is a sticky sheet on which a pheromone pellet is placed. Because this exudes a scent similar to that produced by virgin females, male moths are lured into the trap and get stuck.

NET A CHERRY TO REAP YOUR CROP

Or the birds will eat the fruits before you do, because thirsty birds of all kinds love succulent cherries. For humans, swallowing cherry stones is said to have dire effects.

Netting a large cherry tree may be impractical, however – and even if you manage to throw a small-meshed net over a small tree you risk the birds getting tangled in it if they try to steal your fruit. It may help to place a birdbath near the tree to tempt birds to slake their thirst there instead.

To grow a cherry small enough to net successfully you need a plant grafted on to a dwarfing rootstock such as Gisela 5. Smallest of all are those on Colt rootstocks, which will even thrive in large pots. As for flavour, modern cherries come in two main types: 'sour' cherries related to the morello (*Prunus cerasus*) and 'sweet' cherries descended from the wild cherry or gean (*P. avium*).

> *Swallow them at your peril? Cherry stones have a poor reputation, being said to cause everything from appendicitis to the actual sprouting of a tree in the stomach.*

The traditional 'Cherry Tree Carol' is based on the apocryphal story of Mary and Joseph walking in the garden. Mary asks Joseph to pick her a cherry but he refuses, angry at the news that she is pregnant and he is not the father. However, the tree itself bows down – at the command of the child in her womb – and presents her with the fruit:

> *Then bow'd down the highest tree*
> *Unto his mother's hand:*
> *When she cried, 'See, Joseph,*
> *I have cherries at command!'*

ALWAYS DOUBLE DIG

This advice from the past is by no means universally accepted or advisable today, when many gardeners have positively adopted a 'no dig' policy. The state of your soil – and its type – will be crucial in your choice of method and your timing.

Double digging means digging down to two spade depths, or spits. This is hard work, best done in autumn, but has the advantage, particularly on heavy soil, of allowing roots to penetrate more deeply, especially those of long-rooted plants such as parsnips and runner beans. Double digging also makes it possible to remove the deep roots of perennial weeds and large stones, and to loosen compacted soil, but it is not something you need to do every year. As you dig, fill the trenches with compost or well-rotted manure, but do not bury it too deeply or all its goodness will just leach away.

No-dig gardening should be preceded by thorough double or single digging. The principle is to apply a mulch of compost, either before or after planting, through which plants can grow. Worms, the garden's natural diggers, pull the mulch into the soil.

Single digging is best done in spring and in any event is always preferable to double digging for light soils. Often all you need to do is turn over the top layer of soil to break it up and aerate it, and to remove the weeds, though annual weeds can be easily dug back into the ground, where they will rot and enrich the soil.

> ## THE GARDENER
> *In his 1885 poem, Robert Louis Stevenson portrayed the absorbing task of digging from a child's point of view:*
>
> The gardener does not love to talk,
> He makes me keep the gravel walk;
> And when he puts his tools away,
> He locks the door and takes the key.
>
> Away behind the currant row
> Where no one else but cook may go,
> Far in the plots, I see him dig
> Old and serious, brown and big.

Never mix manure and lime

Because they will largely cancel each other out and waste your efforts. Timing each application correctly, and getting to know the acidity level of your soil, are the keys to the best use of these two important soil improvers.

Lime is the perfect treatment if your soil is sour and too acid. To avoid damage to plants, it is best applied after autumn digging so that it can work its way into the soil over the winter. Well-rotted manure can then be added in the spring to provide nutrients and improve soil texture and water retention. It is best to be cautious with lime. About 200g per sq m (6oz per sq yd) is a reasonable amount to begin with.

On clay soil, lime has an extra benefit. By helping the fine particles of clay amass into small lumps it greatly improves soil drainage. Don't dig lime in: spread it on the surface and let the rain wash it into the ground.

Avoid, at all costs, mixing lime with commercial fertilizer. The alkali and acid can have an explosively damaging effect.

Measuring acidity

Get a soil testing kit and follow the instructions to rate your soil acidity in pH or 'power of hydrogen'. On the pH scale, 7 is neutral, 4 highly acid and 8 alkaline. Most vegetables prefer soil just on the acid side of neutral – around 6.8, though most brassicas like a slightly alkaline reading of just over 7 while potatoes do well at about 6.5. So plan your crops accordingly. Where you have grown potatoes, for example, lime the soil then plant brassicas there the following year.

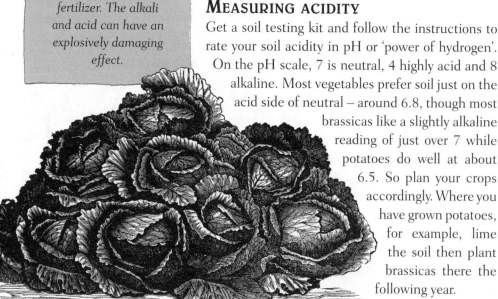

RASPBERRIES HATE DROUGHT

Which is why they need
plenty of mulching,
especially if they are
growing in full sun.
Responding to raspberries'
needs also depends on good timing,
and on whether they fruit early or late.

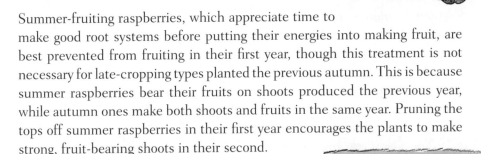

Summer-fruiting raspberries, which appreciate time to
make good root systems before putting their energies into making fruit, are
best prevented from fruiting in their first year, though this treatment is not
necessary for late-cropping types planted the previous autumn. This is because
summer raspberries bear their fruits on shoots produced the previous year,
while autumn ones make both shoots and fruits in the same year. Pruning the
tops off summer raspberries in their first year encourages the plants to make
strong, fruit-bearing shoots in their second.

The fruit-bearing stems of early raspberries should be cut back nearly to the ground after harvesting. By contrast, all the stems of autumn varieties need cutting in early spring, before the new season's shoots emerge. Leaving the tops on until then gives some protection from frost.

Because they are shallow rooted, all raspberries appreciate support, shelter and an absence of weeds, which suck vital water from the soil. A mulch of grass cuttings (ideally mixed with compost to prevent them from getting slimy), bark or very well rotted leaf mould, spread after watering, will help to suppress most weeds, but it needs to be thick to deter persistent perennials.

The raspberry gets the second part of its scientific name (Rubus idaeus) from the fact that it grew copiously on the slopes of Mount Ida. According to legend, the original raspberry was white but the nymph Ida, trying to calm the screams of the infant Zeus, scratched her breast on the raspberry she was picking for him and her blood stained it red.

PLANT PEARS FOR YOUR HEIRS

Pear trees can take up to twenty years to fruit when planted from seed, but can live for well over a century. Since few pears are self-fertile, you will need two plants (they can be different varieties) that flower at the same time to ensure a good crop.

'Natural' ungrafted pear trees can grow to 7m (21ft) or more. The best ones for most modern gardens are those grafted on to quince rootstocks, which keep tree size under control and produce fruit relatively quickly. Compared with apples, pears appreciate more sun and warmth and a more fertile, loamy soil. A sheltered spot will also help to protect the early spring blossom from wind and ensure good pollination. Careful matching of varieties will give you fruit right into winter.

The pear (*Pyrus* spp) originated, with the apple, in the Caucasus and was long considered the superior fruit, especially by the Greeks and Romans. Pliny described as many as 41 varieties. Over the centuries, pears have been bred to create the thousand and more varieties that are now known. For cooking, the Warden pear, which was bred by Cistercian monks in Berkshire in medieval times, and was also known as the Shakespeare, was a kitchen staple until the plethora of breeding in the 16th and 17th centuries that resulted in sweeter, less gritty, eaters.

Pears were first grown in America after the Massachusetts Company imported seeds from England in 1629. The Williams pear, first grown in Berkshire in 1770 by John Stair, is known in America as the Bartlett after Enoch Bartlett, who took it there in the following century. The Seckel, a spicy American pear, is said to have been discovered by a trapper in 1765 on a piece of land he had purchased.

A TRADITIONAL DRINK

Perry, a cider-like drink, has been made from pears for centuries. Following the collapse of the Roman Empire, perry making was well established in France but there is no evidence of it in Britain until the Norman Conquest. Perry reached the height of its popularity in the 1960s in the form of Babycham. Launched by the Somerset brewer Francis Showering in 1953, it was marketed as 'Genuine Champagne Perry', pictured in a wide-rimmed champagne glass and accompanied by the line, 'I'd love a Babycham'.

MORE GARDEN PEARS
'Abbé Fetel' – *an old French variety with a red flush.*
'Doyenne de Comice' – *the best of all pears, juicy and without any gritty texture.*
'Conference' – *long and thin in shape with a good flavour.*
'Louise Bonne de Jersey' – *skin flushes red when the fruit is ripe.*
'Josephine de Malines' – *late fruiting with pink flesh. Best allowed to ripen indoors.*
'Winter Nellis' – *a pear with a spicy flavour but rather rough texture that will keep (though not totally reliably) until spring.*

BLACKCURRANTS ARE GARDEN GLUTTONS

And as such they need masses of feeding if they are to produce fruit reliably year after year, but they are worth growing for health reasons alone – just a dozen blackcurrants contain more vitamin C than two large lemons.

To keep blackcurrants well fed, mulch them with garden compost or well-rotted manure every spring. Set new plants (ideally two-year-old bushes certified free of viral disease) deep into the ground. Maintenance consists of

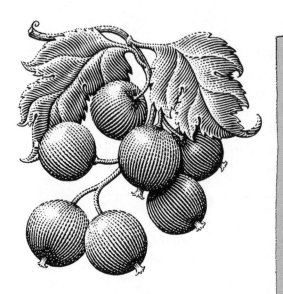

regular pruning of branches that have fruited to make space for young branches to develop. Unlike redcurrants, which fruit on wood of the previous year, blackcurrants fruit on new wood.

The pests you most want to avoid with blackcurrants are the big bud mites (*Cecidophyopsis ribis*). These tiny creatures, which are rarely seen, destroy the buds, making them round and swollen, turning them brown in summer and preventing proper development. This damage is the main cause of so-called reversion disease, for which there is no cure, though picking off and burning swollen buds as soon as you see them is worth trying. The only remedy is to dig up and burn the plants, then plant new ones in a different part of the garden.

YOU CAN'T TRANSPLANT RHUBARB

Not totally true, but you may not be successful if you don't observe the basics of cultivation. A pie, crumble or fool made with early, forced rhubarb is one of the delights that brightens winter's end. In America rhubarb is affectionately known as the 'pie plant'.

Rather than moving rhubarb, it is best to treat it like a herbaceous perennial: dig it up and divide it in either autumn or spring so that the woody parts of the plant can be removed. Otherwise, buy young crowns. Put plenty of manure in the bottom of a deep hole before planting, and add a mulch at least once a year. In the days of horse-drawn transport, children would be sent out to shovel manure from the streets specifically for feeding the garden rhubarb.

PERFECT PINK STEMS

For most practical purposes the best way to force rhubarb is to cover it with a bucket or barrel. Or you can use a special terracotta rhubarb forcer (desirable replicas of Victorian designs are now made) when shoots start to appear early in the year. Straw piled around the base of the forcer will add insulation.

The effects of forcing were discovered by accident at the Chelsea Physic Garden in the early 19th century. The technique was readily adopted by gardeners, who found that the best forcing of all could be achieved in a hothouse with a steady temperature of 12–18°C (55–64°F), with the crowns set in a pit filled with compost. A compost-filled box covered with black plastic mimics this effect.

> Some gardeners are definite in their view that since rhubarb (Rheum rhabarbarum) is grown in the vegetable garden it is not a fruit. Botanically it is classed as a vegetable, but to settle a dispute the US Customs Court in Buffalo, NY, ruled in 1947 that since it was eaten like a fruit, this should be its official description.

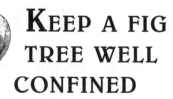

KEEP A FIG TREE WELL CONFINED

An essential measure to restrict the root system and prevent the tree making masses of straggly unproductive growth. One of the most ancient of all cultivated fruits, the fig is a fertility symbol and probably the 'forbidden fruit' eaten by Adam and Eve in the Garden of Eden.

When planting a fig (the best time for this is early spring), restrict its roots by digging a hole just big enough to accommodate them when spread out, then lining it on all sides with bricks. The bottom can be filled with rubble, the tree inserted and the hole filled with soil. A light mulch of compost around the base will complete the operation. Natives of the Mediterranean, figs need a sheltered spot, such as a south-facing wall, as well as some winter protection in chillier areas. The fruits are produced one year and ripen the next, so to help ensure a good crop any fruits that have started to swell, and will not survive the winter, are best removed in early autumn so that the remainder can develop to the full.

The Romans were particularly fond of figs and rated them by quality. The least good were dubbed by Pliny the food of slaves.

The fig plant has an extraordinary means of seed production. The flowers are hidden inside the embryo fruit and are fertilized by female fig wasps, which push their way inside to lay eggs. These duly hatch into male and

In Mediterranean countries the fig is believed to be the spiritual husband of barren women, who are anointed with its sap and tied to the tree in the hope that they will become pregnant.

female larvae, which mate. The impregnated females, now coated with pollen, then force their way out of the fruit and visit another plant to lay their eggs, transporting the pollen and ensuring that the cycle begins again.

Brussels sprouts RELISH HARD GROUND

To get good, tight sprouts it is vital to avoid 'root rock', which is why firm ground suits Brussels sprouts best. This vegetable, a traditional British accompaniment to the Christmas turkey, is one that is either liked or loathed.

To give Brussels sprouts (varieties of *Brassica oleracea*) the best possible conditions, prepare a sheltered spot well in advance. If your soil is light it will need plenty of composting and even then may not be ideal, even if trodden down well. Heavy clay is much more to their liking. They also need plenty of space – allow at least 60cm (2ft) in each direction. Fine netting will give protection from marauding pigeons and cabbage white butterflies.

For a good all-purpose variety choose an F1 hybrid such as 'Breeze', which has smooth, dark green buttons and is a vigorous grower. Of the early hybrids, 'Peer Gynt' is reliable. For sprouts with a difference grow a red variety such as 'Red Bull', whose colour intensifies as the weather grows colder. It is said that you should never pick sprouts until they have had the frost on them, though in fact hard frost can make even the hardiest varieties turn mushy.

Many people hate Brussels sprouts for their strong, slightly sulphurous taste, especially when overcooked. They have a surprisingly different, nutty flavour when finely sliced raw in a salad with grated carrots, apples and mayonnaise.

FOLD THE LEAVES OVER CAULIFLOWER HEADS AS THEY MATURE

A good tip for protecting the curds of summer cauliflowers from the sun and winter cauliflowers from frost. This age-old brassica, dubbed by Mark Twain 'a cabbage with a college education', can be tricky to grow.

A cauliflower is a cabbage (*Brassica oleracea* var. *botrytis cauliflora*) in which flowers begin to form but stop growing while still in bud. There are summer and winter varieties, though technically the latter are actually heading broccoli, not true cauliflowers. For summer cauliflowers you need to sow seed in the previous autumn, then transplant seedlings into a frame or under cloches for overwintering. Harden them off in early spring but wait until the soil has warmed up to plant them out. Keep them well watered and do all you can to keep off attacks from whitefly and cabbage white caterpillars.

Care is essential when transplanting cauliflowers. If not handled with care and planted quickly to the same depth at which they were growing in the frame they will make small, premature heads. Like Brussels sprouts, they need to be firmly rooted and protected from the wind. Winter cauliflowers are less trouble, and can be sown in open ground in spring, then transplanted in early summer.

The origins of the cauliflower are obscure, but it was probably first grown in the Middle East, arriving in Spain in the 12th century. Because the French call it *choux de Chypre* (Cyprus cabbage) the islanders like to claim the vegetable as their own, though the Arabs have a much stronger claim.

Cauliflowers are best cut for the kitchen before the 'curds' begin to open, and it is said that a cauliflower cut soon after daybreak, while it still has the dew on it, tastes best.

NEVER PLANT CABBAGES IN THE SAME PLACE TWO YEARS RUNNING

Or any other brassicas – including broccoli, cauliflowers or Brussels sprouts. One good reason for rotating garden crops is to help keep diseases at bay, including, for brassicas, debilitating club root.

Club root lives up to its name, making roots swollen and distorted and leaves yellow and sickly, although the foliage is perfectly edible. This fungal disease, also called 'finger and toe', strikes during the growing season and severely hampers leaf production. There is no treatment other than to burn affected plants. The best prevention is to treat the soil with hydrated lime at about 240g per sq m (8oz per sq yd) and to add a sprinkling of 4 per cent calomel dust in each hole when seedlings are planted out.

The rotation of crops goes back to the medieval three-field system of farming. Each year one of the fields was ploughed then left fallow to allow it to recover its fertility. Good composting and manuring makes this unnecessary in the average garden, but good drainage, especially of clay soils, always helps vegetable health.

INTERPLANT TO SAVE SPACE

A good idea in all but the largest gardens, and an excellent way of increasing the range of vegetables you can grow. Another way of making the best use of your ground is by catch cropping, which depends on immaculate timing.

True interplanting, or intercropping, means growing crops in close association, with one maturing much more quickly than the other. Lettuces or French beans can be grown between brassicas, summer spinach can be planted between rows of broad beans, and marrows can be planted between potatoes and the shoots trained between the rows. Lettuces will also mature rapidly between rows of maincrop potatoes, though you may need to plant the latter a little more widely to prevent the salad crops being overwhelmed.

In his *Vegetable Grower's Handbook* of 1945, written at a time when wartime food shortages had made maximum cropping paramount, Arthur J. Simmons explained that catch cropping 'consists in snatching a crop off ground which is only vacant for a short period. Obviously,' he continued, 'the crop which is used as a "catch" must itself be quick-growing, or at least must grow more quickly than neighbouring crops.' Today, radishes and rocket make ideal catch crops, as do turnips and beetroot that you intend to eat while still very small and tender.

Even if you are using your space to the full, be sure you have room to hoe and weed properly. Otherwise you will hamper the growth of both crops.

NEVER TRANSPLANT PARSNIP SEEDLINGS

Thinning, not transplanting, is the 'healthy option' for parsnips and other vegetable seedlings that do not respond well to being moved. The leaves of parsnip thinnings are not edible, but the frugal cook will welcome many other vegetable thinnings as additions to seasonal salads and for garnishes.

Parsnips, carrots, beetroot, turnips – and also fennel, pak choi and other varieties of Chinese cabbage – are all much better thinned than transplanted. Transplanting can impair the growth of the plants' roots, leaving you with substandard crops. Although, as with transplanting, nimble fingers are a boon for thinning, the advantage is that thinning can be done in stages, so that you gradually give plants the space they need. And there are few vegetables more tasty than tiny, thinned beetroots served with a mustard sauce (the purple-ribbed leaves also make an excellent ingredient in salads).

Thin while the plants are small, as soon as the seedlings are large enough to be handled with ease. If you leave them too long the roots of adjacent plants will get tangled together. A day when the soil has been well dampened by rain is perfect for the job.

> Parsnips were popular as a vegetable in Europe before the arrival of the potato. They were cultivated by the Romans and were prized for both their sugar content and their high starch content. In medieval times they were often used in boiled plum puddings.

Poor soil makes spinach go to seed

Rather than making tasty, nutritious leaves, flowering is the plant's natural reaction to threat, which may be posed by a shortage of food or water.

When faced with poor conditions, plants of all kinds will quickly flower and seed – so as to be sure of producing the next generation, and this is especially true of annuals. With spinach, light soil low in organic matter is most likely to deprive plants of the moisture they need and to make them bolt, so compost well before sowing seed. As well as plenty of moisture and food – a liquid feed every two weeks is recommended once the plants are beginning to establish – give spinach plenty of room to grow by thinning it out well (use the thinnings in a tasty salad).

For a good succession of spinach, sow regularly: for baby leaves, quick-growing varieties will be ready to crop in just four weeks. To prevent plants running to seed, and to ensure a maximum supply of leaves, it also helps to pick the crop regularly.

Eastern origins

True spinach (*Spinacea oleracea*) gets its name from the old Persian *aspanakh*, reflecting its origin in that country, and it still grows wild in Iran. It was introduced to medieval Europe by the Arabs, and it gradually came to replace less tasty greens such as sorrel and orache, which were largely gathered from the countryside. Spinach was originally used in both sweet and savoury dishes. In Provence, a traditional *tarte d'epinards au sucre* is still eaten on Christmas Eve.

A slip of the pen, perpetrated in the 1870s, gave spinach its reputation as the most iron-rich vegetable. When calculating its iron content a food analyst put a decimal point in the wrong place, implying that the iron content was ten times its real value. The mistake was not rectified until 1937, and not publicized until 1981.

KNOW YOUR GREENS

Choose spinach and its relatives for year-round leaves.

Annual spinach	Best varieties include 'Triathlon', 'Emeila' and 'Trinidad'	Sow from late winter for summer crops, early autumn for overwintering
Perpetual spinach	Look for seeds advertised as mildew resistant	Sow early spring to midsummer
Sea kale (Swiss chard)	Comes in white and crimson-stemmed (rhubarb) varieties	Sow mid-spring to early summer
New Zealand spinach	Grow as an annual	Sow from spring (after frost risk) to midsummer
Good King Henry (fat hen)	Does not respond well to transplantation	Sow in mid-spring

Popeye the sailor, quantity consumer of spinach and possessed of bulging muscles as a result, was created in 1929 by the cartoonist Elzie Crisler Segar. A Popeye statue stands today in Segar's home town of Chester, Illinois.

SOW RADISHES EVERY TEN DAYS

Good advice in spring and summer to ensure a continuous supply of this popular salad vegetable. As well as fast-maturing pink and red summer radishes there are other colours to choose from, including black or Spanish radishes and white oriental types. And some of them can grow to giant proportions.

Summer radishes are easy to grow, and are best sown in small quantities since, once mature, they quickly become woody. Two rows of about 1m (39in) are ample at each sowing. The soil need not be deeply dug, but should not be recently manured. Classic summer varieties, including the old white-tipped favourite 'French Breakfast', can be started under cloches, or even outdoors in a sunny spot as early as midwinter.

According to the Greek historian Herodotus, the Great Pyramid bore an inscription attesting to the vast quantities of radishes (and onions and garlic) eaten by the construction force.

Winter radishes, with long or turnip-shaped roots that can weigh 250g (8oz) and more, take longer to mature and need soil that is more deeply dug. Seed sowing is from early to late summer. It is now also easy to obtain seeds of the white Japanese radish – known as the daikon or mooli – hybridized for garden excellence and its mild, peppery flavour.

It is said that radishes that have been pulled up during a waning moon will, if rubbed on the affected part, cure both corns and warts. Radishes are also notorious for provoking indigestion.

MIND WHERE YOU PUT MINT

Because it will run riot if left unconfined and may be best grown in a large pot or tub. Several mints, however, make quick 'fillers' for the border.

A good way to stop mint spreading is to restrict the roots by planting it in an old biscuit tin (with drainage holes pierced in the base) then sink the tin into the soil. If you want to grow mints of different varieties, such as the dark-leaved eau de cologne mint or the variegated pineapple mint, they can be planted in a group or placed as you wish around the garden. If you want to grow just one variety the soft, hairy-leaved apple mint (*Mentha suaveolens*) is a good choice.

Less invasive and more tender than regular mints is the purple-flowered pennyroyal mint (*M. pulegium*), which gets its name from the custom of using it to repel the king's fleas. It was a medieval custom to plunge a bunch of pennyroyal into water to purify it, though it was also believed to be used by witches to make malignant potions.

Smallest of all mints is the Corsican mint (*M. requienii*), which has single purple flowers. It will enhance any rock garden or can be planted between the stones in a path, where its aroma will be released with your footfall.

Mints get their scientific name from the nymph Mintha. According to legend she was loved by the god Hades but was turned into a mint plant by his jealous wife Persephone.

Plant courgette seeds on their sides

A ruse that will encourage good germination, as will soaking seeds in water overnight before they are planted. For gourmets, courgettes (zucchini) are as valuable for their flowers, which are traditionally stuffed and deep fried, as for their fruits.

Like other tender vegetables, courgettes need warmth for reliable germination, and should not be planted out until the risk of frosts is passed and each plant has at least two true leaves (not just the oval seed leaves). Put single seeds into small deep pots or cells, or two per larger pot.

Once established, courgettes will rapidly produce foliage, flowers and fruit, though they are ready targets for slugs and snails. Until fruits begin to form they should be allowed to dry out before being watered. Too much water will encourage leaves rather than fruits.

Judging the right moment to pick courgettes is tricky. Fruits that look not quite large enough one day can swell to overgrown proportions overnight. For showing under Royal Horticultural Society rules, fruits – with flowers attached – should measure no more than 15cm (6in) in length. Frequent harvesting helps avoid small fruits rotting, as plants struggle to balance their resources.

Botanically, courgettes are closely related to marrows and like them produce both male and female flowers. Early in the season, when daylength is still short, the plants may produce many more male than female flowers, and it may help to hand pollinate, simply by rubbing a male flower against a female one.

A matter of language: the name courgette comes from the French, zucchini from the Italian (and it was the Italians who introduced the vegetable to the USA). But even in the 1920s it was known in France as la courgette d'Italie.

FOR BETTER TOMATOES, PINCH OUT SIDE SHOOTS

Good advice for many types of tomatoes, but by no means all. Bush tomatoes do not need this treatment, and removing side shoots will reduce the size of the crop.

There are few more pleasurable experiences than picking and eating a tomato direct from the vine and still warm from the sun. Even if you have no greenhouse and limited space outdoors it is well worth making room to cultivate tomatoes. The breeders have helped too, by creating varieties that ripen much more reliably than in the past. They are extraordinarily versatile, especially if you grow them in pots or growing bags. They can be placed against a sunny wall at the back of a flower border, or grown on a windowsill. And there are new varieties bred specifically for growing in hanging baskets.

Tomato plants usually begin to make side shoots when they are some 20–30cm (8–12in) tall. To help quell re-growth, wait until side shoots are about 25mm (1in) long before pinching them out. When the plants are growing strongly you will need to do this every two or three days. Once four or six good trusses have formed, 'stop' each plant by pinching out the top.

Apart from blight (see page 187) tomatoes are prone to other problems. Young plants allowed to become too wet will grow weak and sappy and be prone to diseases. If established plants are allowed to get too wet or too dry flowers may drop or fruit, if it does form, may develop ugly splits. Regular feeding is essential, but given too much nitrogen the leaves will begin to curl. An old-fashioned method is to line the bottoms of planting holes with a layer of nettles. As the nettles decompose they release nitrogen to the roots of the tomato plants.

GREEN TOMATOES

If you have unripened green tomatoes left at the end of the season, do not discard them. They not only make excellent chutney, but are very tasty in stir-fried dishes with hot spices. Alternatively, try wrapping them individually in tissue paper and putting them into a drawer or cardboard box with a few ripe tomatoes or a couple of bananas. This way, you may have good fruit well into the autumn.

TOMATO CHOICES

Select some of these varieties for great tomato crops in any position in the garden.

For the greenhouse	'Beefeater' – large fruited 'Red Shine', 'Shirley' – medium sized 'Tropical Ruby' – small fruited
Outdoors – and will also do well under glass, need pinching out	'Ailsa Craig'. 'Moneymaker', 'Alicante', 'Vandos', 'Harlequin', 'Yellow Perfection'
Bush types for outdoors or indoors, no pinching out needed	'Sweet Million', 'Totem', 'Mirabelle'
For hanging baskets and containers	'Tumbler', 'Tumbling Tom Yellow', 'Balconi Red'

IT TAKES NINETY DAYS TO GROW A LETTUCE FROM SEED

If not exactly, this is approximately correct, though there are ways to speed up the growing time. This most popular salad leaf has been cultivated, not least for medical purposes, for at least 6,000 years.

The challenge for the lettuce grower is to achieve a steady supply of salad leaves all year, without gaps or gluts. From early spring to midsummer, seed can be sown outdoors and, protected by cloches or horticultural fleece, will mature in less than three months. Planting small quantities every three weeks works reasonably well as long as you are able to keep your lettuces well watered. If they get dry they will bolt quickly. Fleece helps again here, as it conserves water around the plants. For very early crops, hardy over-wintering varieties such as 'Valdor' can be sown in early autumn, while 'All the Year Round', sown in late summer and kept frost free, will mature at the beginning of winter.

CHOICE OF LEAF

Lettuce (*Lactuca sativa*) comes in three types. The cos or romaine lettuces, with crisp, oval leaves; the round-headed cabbage lettuces, including butterhead, iceberg and crisp heart; and loose-leaved lettuces such as 'Salad Bowl', which produce no heart and from which leaves can be cropped for several months.

> Lettuce sap contains substances that help promote sleep. In the 'soporific sponge', a medieval attempt at anaesthesia, it was mixed with the more powerful hemlock, poppy and mandrake.

LEEKS ARE GREEDY FEEDERS

These vegetables certainly need plenty of food if they are to grow to a generous size, though the champion growers of giant leeks in Britain's northeast guard their secret fertilizer formulae closely.

Rich, fertile soil, well composted during late autumn, is the starting point for a good leek crop, but these vegetables also appreciate a dressing of superphosphate given at 30g per sq m (1oz per sq yd) and potassium sulphate at half that dosage, lightly forked into the soil in late spring before pencil-thick young plants about 20cm (8in) tall are set out.

Leeks fare well when planted out the traditional way: make dibber holes about 6in (15cm) deep and drop the plants in. Water them well but do not fill the hole with soil. Some gardeners trim the tops to cut down water loss, but this is really only necessary in very hot weather. As the leeks grow, feed them regularly with a liquid feed or top dress with concentrated manure, then in autumn, earth up the plants to maximize the length of the white part of each plant.

Champion leek growers tend their plants individually, setting them at least 30cm (12in) apart and growing specimens that can weigh more than 4.5kg (9lb) with stems measuring over 7.5cm (3in) in diameter.

To get leeks that are big and fat it is said that they should be planted when the moon is waxing. Set them out during a waning moon, and you will have plants that are small and sour.

Hippocrates prescribed leeks as a remedy for nosebleeds, and for the Romans the leek was the most prized member of the onion family. The Emperor Nero, who believed that eating them would clear his voice and improve his singing, ate leeks in such quantity that he was nicknamed Porrophagus, 'the leek eater'.

Be careful – you'll never get rid of horseradish

Good advice, because while horseradish is one of the easiest plants to grow it is also vigorous and invasive – once allowed to spread it is almost impossible to eradicate. But there is nothing better with roast beef than the fresh root.

Horseradish (*Armoracia rusticana*) is native to southeast Europe but was growing wild in England by the mid-16th century. Lightly crushing the leaves produces the unmistakable aroma. The best way of cultivating – and confining – it is to grow it in pieces of drainpipe about 2ft (60cm) long, pushed into the ground and filled with a mixture of compost and soil. In early spring plant a piece of root, ideally 6–12in (15–30cm) long, in each container. As the roots mature you can use them as needed. In late autumn the remaining crop is best lifted and the roots stored in boxes of peat through the winter. From these will come the roots to start off next year's crop. If horseradish escapes and spreads, your only solution may be to kill it with weedkiller, let the ground recover and start again.

Horseradish sauce is the traditional accompaniment to roast beef, England's 'national' dish. The ingredients of the sauce are fresh horseradish, grated just before using (to preserve its natural oils and therefore its pungency), stirred with vinegar to give the consistency of cream, plus sugar, salt, pepper and mustard powder.

Medically, horseradish has long been used to stimulate the appetite and as a treatment for kidney stones. A country remedy for the pain of rheumatism is a poultice made from grated horseradish root.

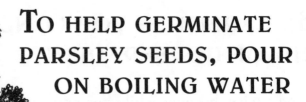

TO HELP GERMINATE PARSLEY SEEDS, POUR ON BOILING WATER

You can do this after the seeds have been planted to help speed the notoriously slow germination of this garden herb, which can take up to 70 or even 90 days. In the parsley bed – as well as under the gooseberry bush – is the place where babies are said to come from.

Other good tips for parsley are to soak the seeds in warm water before they are put into the ground, or to start them off indoors and transplant the seedlings later, though many people think that this is unlucky – even an omen of death. As to variety, the cooks' choice is the taller flat-leaved or 'continental' type *Petroselinum crispum* var. *neapolitanum*, also known as French parsley, which they believe has more flavour than the curly-leaved cultivars. When supplies of the curly-leaved herb are abundant, revive the old favourite of deep-fried parsley. Immerse it for just 15 seconds in hot fat, until it turns deep green and crisp.

Parsley can be found growing wild in southern Europe. Although the Romans gathered and used it they probably did not use it in the kitchen; they planted it deliberately only on graves, hence its association with ill fortune. It reached British gardens and tables in the mid-16th century, though it was especially commended for flavour by the Emperor Charlemagne some 800 years before that.

> 'Where parsley grows faster,' say the superstitious, 'the mistress is master.' In other words, the woman rules the roost. The plant is also said to grow better when seeds are planted by a woman.

CHIT POTATOES 'NOSE END' UPWARDS

The correct positioning for getting the best sprouts on your tubers. For the earliest crops, you should begin chitting in late winter and plant out six weeks later. For main crop potatoes, later chitting is fine, as long as you do not allow the tubers to become overheated.

Letting potatoes sprout or 'chit' before planting is the best way to ensure the highest yield. Ideally, place the potatoes with their thickest ends uppermost in slatted trays in a cool dry place, but make sure they have some light, or they will sprout weak, spindly shoots.

At planting time, rub off all but the best one or two sprouts with your thumb to concentrate the growth effort of the plant. You can plant in a trench or use a bulb planter to make holes into which individual potatoes can be set. To help prevent the tubers from developing too near the surface and turning green, earth up the rows after planting, then again once the top growth appears – and continue to do so fortnightly until the flowers open.

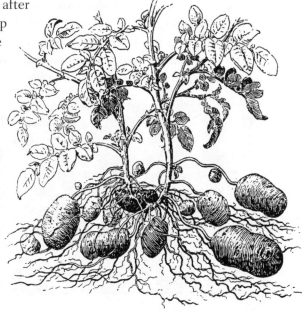

For variety in the kitchen, try growing some unusual 'heritage' potato varieties such as 'Red Duke of York' (first earlies) or purple 'Edzell Blue' (second earlies). For a main crop there are still few potatoes to better the good old-fashioned 'King Edward'.

Keep chicory in the dark

Excluding light is essential for the pale heads or 'chicons' that grow from the roots when kept in the dark. Other types of chicory, also confusingly known as endive, do not need this treatment.

Seeds of 'Witloof' chicory (*Cichorum intybus*) can be sown outdoors in early summer in any well-cultivated soil. In mid-autumn, dig up the roots and cut off the crowns. Then plant the roots, closely packed, into boxes or pots of loamy soil, water well, and cover them so that no light will penetrate. Kept warm – the temperature should never be any lower than about 7°C (45°F) – the chicons will form in four to six weeks.

> When coffee was first enjoyed in Europe it was extremely expensive, and from the 18th century roasted chicory root was commonly substituted for the real thing. In France and Spain a mixture of coffee and chicory is still popular.

Endives (*C. endivia*), close relatives of chicory, also benefit from some light exclusion, but in a different way. Grow the plants like other salad vegetables then, when mature, tie the leaves loosely with raffia and cover the whole plant with a large pot to create a white heart and reduce bitterness. Be sure to cover the drainage hole in the pot for total light exclusion.

Beyond white

Not all chicory is white – or called chicory:
- **Sugarloaf** – green, leafy chicory.
- **Catalogna** – also called asparagus chicory – has leaves with thick white stalks.
- **Radicchio** – red-leaved chicory that does not need blanching.
- **Frisée** – a broad-leaved variety of endive with frizzy leaves, also known as Batavia and escarole.

Herbs flourish on poor soil

Many do, because these are the conditions that prevail in their natural habitats, though some, like parsley and chervil, need rich soil and are treated like leafy vegetables. Above all, most herbs need excellent drainage and plenty of sunshine.

The herbs that are natives of the Mediterranean, including rosemary, sage, thyme and oregano, are the ones that do best in poor soil. In a sunny position they will grow strong and compact, and the oils in their leaves, which give them their distinctive aromas, will become wonderfully concentrated.

Although they are key ingredients in the kitchen, herbs certainly do not need to be confined to the vegetable garden. Some species, such as angelica, bronze-leaved fennel and variegated thyme, are a positive asset in the herbaceous border, while chives – both ordinary and garlic chives – make excellent border edgings. Both green and purple-leaved basils make a strong, leafy statement among other annuals, though they will be most productive if they are not allowed to flower. Dill can also accompany other annuals in the flower garden.

During the Middle Ages, healing herbs were called 'simples' and herbalists were known as 'simplers'. Sage (Salvia officinalis) is named from the Latin salveo meaning 'I am well' – a tribute to its many healing properties.

4. HEALTHY TREES AND SHRUBS

Trees and shrubs are the backbone of the garden – the 'skeleton' on which the rest of the design is built and nurtured. They are also a source of garden delight, from the wonderful scents of roses and lilacs to the brilliant yellow of the forsythia blooms that herald the arrival of spring, and the musty scent of freshly clipped box on a summer's evening.

Both shrubs and trees – but particularly trees – can cause problems if they grow too large. While old gardening books wax lyrical about the merits of everything from weeping willows to Douglas firs, they reflect an age in which gardens were generally much larger than they are now, and when many gardens included large trees that were decades if not centuries old. Yet new trees are our own legacy for generations to come, for, as the old saying goes, 'He that plants trees loves others beside himself.'

Hedges, whose origin lies in the dividing up of farmland, are now garden staples and have always provoked arguments between garden neighbours, none more so than the infamous Leyland cypress. But there are many wonderful old-fashioned shrubs that not only make excellent hedges but will be welcomed for both shelter and as nesting sites for the birds that bring so much pleasure to garden owners – just as long as they are not attacking their precious fruit.

GROW BUDDLEIAS FOR BUTTERFLIES

Of all garden shrubs these are undoubtedly the strongest magnets for butterflies – and moths. Their attraction is the nectar at the base of each of the tiny tube-shaped flowers that make up the densely packed, elongated flower head.

Buddleias are easy to grow. The species form *B. davidii* quickly colonizes waste ground, growing in small cracks in paving and on walls. For superabundance of butterflies, however, the best choices are the pale lilac types, such as 'Lochinch', 'Les Kneale' and 'Dartmoor'.

The buddleia is native to China and is named for the Reverend Adam Buddle, a plant collector who died in 1715. *B. davidii* gets its name from the Jesuit missionary Abbé Armand David, who discovered it in 1869.

In the garden, buddleias can quickly become straggly and get out of hand. Because they flower on new season's growth it is best to cut them down almost to ground level at the end of winter. If the spent brown flower heads are regularly removed, new lateral blooms will be produced, extending the flowering season well into autumn.

BUTTERFLY LORE

Butterflies are regarded as both good and bad, depending on circumstances, and beliefs are often contradictory:

- *Butterflies are witches in disguise – or a soul returned to earth.*
- *For good luck kill the first butterfly you see in spring, or catch it and let it fly through your sleeve.*
- *If the first butterfly of the year is yellow it heralds a birth, if white a death.*
- *If the first butterfly you see is white, then you will eat white bread all year. If brown, then it will be brown bread (once a sign of poverty).*

WISTERIA IS WORTH WAITING FOR

It can take up to a decade for a wisteria to begin to bloom, but there are few plants more delightful as decoration for the front of a house. Wisterias have been prized in Japan since at least the eighth century.

Plant choice and attention to pruning are two essentials of success with wisterias. When buying a plant, select one that has been grafted on to an existing rootstock, rather than grown from seed. It will be more reliable and bloom sooner. In late summer each year, cut back long, non-flowering shoots to five or six leaves from their base. Then, in winter, reduce these to just two buds.

A wisteria will do best in a south-facing position in soil that is well nourished with potash. Be sure to avoid providing too much nitrogen, which will encourage the growth of leaves rather than flowers. The shrub's decorative virtues for a 'fine house' were extolled by the influential gardener Gertrude Jekyll: '… a wisteria judiciously placed, carefully trained and restricted to a few level lines, is often helpful, and very beautiful with its clear-cut foliage and drooping clusters of light purple blooms.'

> All wisterias climb, but they do not all do so in the same direction. While *W. floribunda* climbs clockwise, *W. sinensis* grows anticlockwise. Left unpruned, both can reach heights of 40m (130ft).

Wisteria, native to East Asia, was introduced to the West from China in 1816. Though it was named in honour of the American physician and professor of anatomy Caspar Wistar (1761–1818), 'wisteria' and not 'wistaria' is the officially approved spelling.

A VIGOROUS HEDGE MAY MAKE A BAD NEIGHBOUR

A saying that most surely relates to the rampant hybrid Leyland cypress (x *Cupressocyparis leylandii*) but could also apply to any hedge that is allowed to get out of control. There are many more attractive choices that are much less bothersome.

Hedges originated in England as a means of sectioning off pieces of agricultural land. They were a valuable source of firewood and also provided a shield against wind and rain, both for livestock and for the men and women out working in the fields. Even in the 18th century, foreign visitors to England marvelled at them, commenting that they 'make the whole countryside seem a beautiful garden'.

GARDEN CHOICES

Apart from leylandii, conifers that make good, dense hedges include the feathery *Thuja* (arborvitae) and *Tsuga canadensis* (eastern hemlock), whose needle-like leaves are often pure white underneath, giving a shimmering effect. Yew, though it may not be to everyone's liking, is ideal if you want to try your hand at topiary (see page 129).

Much more attractive is a hedge that flowers, or produces stunning berries in autumn – or both. For maximum year-round impact choose a hip-bearing rose such as a rugosa, a pyracantha or a euonymus (spindle). *Euonymus alatus*, the winged spindle, is particularly lovely in autumn when the orange seeds inside its open fruits contrast with its vivid red leaves.

> The proverb 'Love your neighbour, yet pull not down your hedge' is a reminder of the usefulness of the hedge in allowing you to keep your distance from the people in the house next door.

As a hedge establishes itself, keep it well watered and trim it so that long thin shoots are never allowed to develop. Cutting little and often is much better in the early stages than drastic pruning once a year. As the hedge grows, trim it so that the base is always wider than the top.

A FUCHSIA MAKES A CHARMING HEDGE

These beautiful shrubs do, indeed, make excellent hedges in mild areas, but while popular all over Ireland are not widely seen elsewhere. From the shape of their flowers, fuchsias are commonly known as 'ladies' eardrops'.

Each fuchsia flower consists of a central bell of petals around which are four sepals, and these form the flower's tubular base. From the middle of the petal group, which may be single, double or semi-double, prominent stamens emerge. But no botanical description can do justice to these complex but delicate flowers. The great Victorian gardener William Robinson was a fuchsia enthusiast. 'Its full beauty,' he said, 'is seen when we use plants with rather tall stems or pyramids. In the milder districts where it is a shrub, we see it to perfection … if used judiciously they give an air of grace afforded by no other plants.'

Of all the hardy fuchsias, *Fuchsia* 'Ricartonii' is one of the best to choose for a

Like many plants, fuchsias are named for a scientist of note: Leonhart Fuchs was the author of the most meritorious herbal of his day. However, the plant was not named until 1703, 137 years after his death.

hedge. Other vigorous hedging selections include *F. denticulata*, which can top 4m (13ft) in a few years; its flowers have orange petals and red sepals. For a smaller hedge you could try the low-growing *F.* 'Madame Cornelissen', which will reach a height of about 1.2m (4ft). It has pretty semi-double scarlet and white flowers.

FANTASTIC FUCHSIAS

In addition to hardy fuchsias there are dozens of half-hardy varieties, which are ideal for bedding and growing in pots, as well as trailing fuchsias for hanging baskets. Some, such as the golden-leaved 'Autumnale', also have attractive foliage. For a rockery or unusual ground cover there is also *F. procumbens*, with pale orange flowers and dark green heart-shaped leaves.

Most impressive of all are standard fuchsias, whose single, woody stems are encouraged to grow in the greenhouse, supported by canes. Side shoots are removed until the plant is the required height, at which point the growing point is pinched out and growth controlled by further pinching until a round head is created.

GROWING TIPS FOR FUCHSIAS

- *Leave hardy fuchsias unpruned until spring to protect against frost. Protect plant bases with piles of dead bracken or fallen leaves.*
- *Take softwood fuchsia cuttings in midsummer when the plant is in full leaf. Ideally use a non-flowering shoot and remove the lower pairs of leaves. Keep warm and well watered. Take cuttings from semi-matured wood in late summer and early autumn.*
- *Dig up and divide large plants in spring.*
- *Overwinter half-hardy fuchsias in a frost-free place. Until mid-spring, water only if stems appear to be drying out, then water well to stimulate new growth.*
- *Deadhead the plants regularly to encourage more flowers and to keep them looking tidy.*
- *Rather than mulching them, which will encourage foliage at the expense of flowers, feed fuchsias with a weak manure solution.*

You may weep for a willow

You surely will if you choose one that is too big for your garden. Perfect when young and small, it may rapidly take over the entire space. Gardeners often misjudge the potential dimensions of weeping willows.

There are so many willows to choose from that it is perfectly possible to find one that will suit the size of your garden. You need a large space to indulge in the weeping, golden-leaved *Salix* x *sepulcralis* var. *chrysocoma*, which can attain a height and spread of 15m (50ft) or more. For a small garden a safer choice is a dwarf form of the goat willow (*S. caprea pendula*), though for showy catkins you need to select the male form 'Kilmarnock'.

Contorted or corkscrew willows, also called dragon's claw willows, are dramatic garden specimens with branches that twist and turn, making superb sculptural shapes. *S. babylonica* var. *pekinensis* var. *tortuosa* will reach about 10m (33ft) in 15 years, but it can also be grown – and kept in check – in a large pot. Pussy willow, named from its silky soft spring catkins is, most usually, *S. caprea* in Europe and *S. discolor* in the USA. As well as gracing the garden its branches are superb for indoor arrangements.

Willow pattern is the distinctive blue and white pottery that was based on a Chinese design and first produced in England around 1780 by Thomas Turner. The pattern depicts the legend of the mandarin Li-chi and his only daughter, Koong-she, who eloped by boat with Chang, the mandarin's lowly secretary. The mandarin chased after the pair, but the gods changed them into a pair of turtle doves.

ALLOW MAGNOLIAS ROOM TO EXPAND

These beautiful additions to any garden need plenty of space to grow, both above and below ground. Many magnolias herald the spring with flowers that emerge before the leaves. As they mature, they produce more and more flowers every year.

Among the largest of all the magnolias is the magnificent evergreen *Magnolia grandiflora* – the southern magnolia or bull bay – which bears its huge creamy flowers with a lemony scent from midsummer to early autumn. Reaching at least 15m (50ft) in height, it will do best against a sunny house wall where it will be protected from the wind. An American native, it is the state flower of both Mississippi and Louisiana – and the former is officially nicknamed the Magnolia State.

Less huge is the deciduous lily tree or yulan (*M. denudata*), whose white flowers, appearing before the foliage, are tinged with pink. If you want flowers quickly – and can afford it – buy a magnolia that is about five years old. Until this age they produce few if any blooms.

PLANT FAMILIES

Linnaeus named the magnolia for Pierre Magnol (1638–1715), because 'it is handsome both in foliage and flower, and worthy of so fine a man'. Magnol was a renowned French botanist and director of the Botanic Gardens in Montpellier; with Linnaeus, he is remembered as one of the inventors of the system of plant classification we use today, as it was he who conceived the idea of plant 'families'.

Lovers have traditionally used fallen magnolia petals to send messages to each other. 'Writing' with a pin damages the white petal and turns it brown, causing the words to emerge.

IF YOU PLANT ONLY ONE THING IN YOUR GARDEN, MAKE IT A TREE

A splendid sentiment. Not only will a tree enhance your garden but it will also become a living heirloom for many future generations.

There are so many delightful trees to choose for the garden, as Chaucer made plain in *The Parliament of Fowls*, listing their practical uses too:

> *The builder oak, and eke the hardy ash,*
> *The pillar elm, the coffin unto carrain;*
> *The box, pipe tree, the holm to whippes lash,*
> *The sailing fir, the cypress, death to playne;*
> *The shooter yew, the asp for shaftes plain,*
> *The olive of peace, and eke the drunken vine,*
> *The victor palm, the laurel to divine.*

For today's gardener, the most important consideration is usually the size to which a tree will grow. Weeping willows (see page 109) are notorious for outgrowing their allotted space, but the same applies to many other species. For this reason it is best to take expert advice before making a final choice. A good nursery will not only suggest good selections for your soil and space but will also plant the tree for you if you wish. Decide, too, whether you are most interested in the tree shape, in having spring flowers and leaves or whether you prefer stunning autumn colour. Or you may want a tree that provides an edible harvest, such as a pear, plum, apple or fig.

ALL ABOUT PLANTING
Positioning is all-important, particularly relative to the house, whose foundations can subside if a tree draws too much water from the surrounding soil. As a rule of thumb, reckon that the roots will spread one and a half times the tree's eventual height – or at least as wide as the widest part of its crown.

Also take note of the shadow it will cast at various times of day. For deciduous trees, plant between autumn and early spring, but conifers are better set into the ground in spring when the soil is both warm and wet. If planted in midwinter they may drop all their foliage and fail to thrive.

When planting, a hole at least 45cm (18in) deep and 1m (3ft) across will be needed for a tree that is three to four years old. Loosen the soil at the bottom of the hole, then add plenty of well-rotted compost to aid drainage and maximize the tree's food supply. A rubber tree strap attached to a stake – or some other means of support that will not damage the trunk – is essential for a newly planted tree to keep the roots firmly in place, whatever the assaults of the wind and weather.

WHY PLANT A TREE?

Some words of wisdom from down the ages:

- 'Men seldom plant trees till they begin to be Wise, that is, till they grow Old and find by Experience the Prudence and Necessity of it.' (John Evelyn 1664).
- 'I never knew before the full value of trees. My house is entirely embosomed in high plain trees, with good grass below, and under them I breakfast, dine, write, read and receive my company.' (Thomas Jefferson, 1807)
- 'A garden without trees scarcely deserves to be called a garden.' (Canon Henry Ellacombe, 1895)
- 'I think that I shall never see/A poem as lovely as a tree.' (Joyce Kilmer, early 1900s)
- 'A good gardener should have ... Solomon's knowledge of all trees, from the cedar to the hyssop.' (S. Reynolds Hole, Dean of Rochester, 1899)

Don't use tapwater on azaleas

The key to this reliable piece of advice is that azaleas are acid lovers. Most tap water contains enough lime to make it alkaline and so endanger the health of these loveliest of spring blooms.

What azaleas like most of all is rainwater, which in cities may even be slightly acid because carbon dioxide in the air dissolves in moisture in the atmosphere to make a very dilute solution of carbonic acid. For azaleas growing indoors, boiled and cooled water is a good alternative. They need plenty of humus and appreciate an annual feed with a specially formulated soil enricher for acid-loving plants. If you adore azaleas but don't have acid soil, then grow them in large pots filled with an acid peat mixed with composted leaf mould, garden soil or grit.

Azaleas are not a species in their own right but a type of rhododendron, usually with scented orange, yellow, pink or white flowers, and deciduous or evergreen foliage. First in cultivation were the deciduous Ghent azaleas, bred from 1815 from seeds of *Rhododendron arboretum* gathered in Nepal.

Before the development of soil-testing kits, gardening was much more a matter of trial and error than it is today, but a dark peaty 'woodland' soil in a garden was a good sign that azaleas and rhododendrons would flourish.

The first azalea seeds to be sent to the West were packed in tins of brown sugar at the Calcutta Botanical Garden by Nathaniel Wallich, the garden's director.

THE BEST BRANCH HAS A PERFECT COLOUR

As does the trunk. Colour is a key consideration when you are choosing trees and shrubs that will grace the garden, especially in winter, though the trunks and branches of trees such as silver birches will enhance your garden all year.

The silver birch (*Betula pendula*) owes its distinctive appearance to the fact that its mature bark peels off in long, papery strips, exposing the fresh young bark beneath. The paper-bark maple (*Acer griseum*) also has peeling bark, but in shades of brown with dazzling orange beneath. Bright red branches are the prime asset of *Salix alba britzensis*, the red willow, while the branches of *Salix daphnoides* are a wonderful purplish violet with a blue bloom. The striped maple (*Acer pensylvanicum* 'Erythrocladum') has young shoots of a brilliant pink, which, as they age, become striped in white.

WINTER COLOUR
Of all the shrubs grown for their winter hues, the best known are the dogwoods, such as *Cornus alba* 'Sibirica', the red-barked dogwood. Most or all o f the stems of these shrubs need to be cut down to ground level in early spring each year for the best colours.

> *A birch broom or besom will rid a house of witches, and burning birch on the fire is said to keep thunder at bay. The inner bark of the birch, mixed with cod oil, is a Newfoundland treatment for frostbite.*

REJUVENATE A HONEYSUCKLE WITH SEVERE PRUNING

This vigorous climber, which can be a garden nuisance if left to its own devices, quickly springs back into life when pruned. Honeysuckles are unfussy about soil and, though they prefer sun, will often do well in partially shaded spots.

Every gardener should find space for a honeysuckle, with its unsurpassed scent. Plant it near a window to perfume your home. Most are tough and unfussy, and some, such as *Lonicera japonica*, are evergreen. Yellow, white, red and cream are the predominant colours in the best garden blooms, many of which have purple buds and undersides. Most are followed by red or black berries, which birds enjoy in autumn. Hard to beat, however, is the European native honeysuckle (*L. periclymenum*), also known to country folk as the woodbine – though the latter is also a name for bindweed.

SCENTED SHRUBS

Some garden honeysuckles are not climbers at all but bushy, versatile shrubs. Species well worth growing are the winter-flowering *L. fragrantissima* and, for an unusual ground cover or to grace a rockery, *L. pileata*.

'Sleep thou, and I will wind thee in my arms.
Fairies, be gone, and be all ways away.
So doth the woodbine and the sweet honeysuckle
Gently entwist; the female ivy so
Enrings the barky fingers of the elm.'
Shakespeare, A Midsummer Night's Dream

Or, where you have room for a plant to sprawl, choose the unusual *L. rupicola* var. *syringantha*, which bears its delicate pink flowers twice a year.

GROW A CLEMATIS OVER A LILAC

For the good reason that once its sweet-scented flowers have faded the lilac can be a tedious, somewhat unattractive plant. But the two plants need to flower at different times of year to allow each to be displayed to perfection.

Like the common species (*Syringa vulgaris*), most lilacs flower in late spring, so the best choices for clematis to grow over them are those that flower in late summer or even in winter while the lilac is still leafless. Many of the best garden lilacs are varieties of the common lilac, though a notable exception is the smaller Persian lilac (*S. x persica*), a relative of the earliest plants brought to Europe from the Middle East in the 1590s.

SYMBOL OF SPRING

Spring is known to some gardeners as 'lilac-tide'. The 19th-century American poet Oliver Wendell Holmes wrote, 'When lilacs blossom, Summer cries "Bud, little roses, Spring is here"', and lilac is cited as the quintessence of spring in the refrain of Ivor Novello's 1945 wartime classic:

> *We'll gather lilacs in the spring again*
> *And walk together down an English lane*
> *Until our hearts have learned to sing again,*
> *When you come home once more.*

To American country folk the lilac was originally known as the laylock. Since 1919 it has been the state flower of New Hampshire: after being brought to

CLEMATIS CHOICES

To grow over a lilac try one of these magnificent clematis:

C. flammula	Clouds of white star-shaped flowers in late summer and autumn
C. viticella 'Abundance'	Pink-red flowers with prominent green stamens from midsummer to mid-autumn
C. cirrhosa 'Freckles'	Cream flowers speckled with purple appear from midwinter to early spring
C. 'Gipsy Queen' (Jackmanii group)	Large deep purple flowers in late summer
C. 'Gravetye Beauty' (Texensis group)	Unusual scarlet small-petalled flowers

And for lilacs try some of these beauties:

Pale to mid-purple	*S. vulgaris 'Michel Buchner', S. x persica*
Deep purple	*S. vulgaris 'Katherine Havemeyer'*
White	*S. vulgaris 'Madame Lemoine'*
Rose pink	*S. microphylla 'Superba'*
Purple-pink	*S. reflexa*

North America from England in the 18th century, it was so widely planted that it became typical of this part of the USA.

In many parts of the world it is thought unlucky to bring lilac blooms indoors. White lilac is considered to be the most malign, even capable of bringing death to the household.

In the language of flowers, a purple lilac bloom means 'you are my first love', but white lilac symbolizes innocence and is a tribute to both beauty and spirituality.

PLANT CLEMATIS WITH THEIR HEADS IN THE SUN AND THEIR ROOTS IN THE SHADE

They love the sun, and will thrive on a south-facing wall, but clematis certainly prefer shade around their roots. These garden favourites now come in so many varieties that it is possible to have one in bloom in every season.

Clematis appreciates careful planting, with the base of the stem about 15cm (6in) below the soil surface to encourage more shoots to emerge from below ground. Fatal to clematis is wilt, a fungus that rots the stems. The threat is greatest in the first two years – before plants have grown wilt-resistant woody stems – and to early-flowering varieties. Hot, humid weather makes a plant especially vulnerable. The only possible cure is to cut away all diseased leaves and stems, water in a fungicide and feed well to encourage new growth.

PRUNING GUIDE

Use this handy rule of thumb:
- *If a clematis flowers early, cut it back immediately after flowering.*
- *If it flowers in mid-season, wait to prune until early spring, and do not be severe.*
- *If it flowers late in the year, prune in early spring, but cut the plant to about 30cm (1ft) from the ground.*

COUNTRY NAMES

Wild clematis (*Clematis vitalba*) is called traveller's joy or old man's beard for the white, fluffy fruits that appear in late autumn and last all winter. It grows in particular profusion along the Pilgrim's Way running from London to Canterbury. It is known in France as *herbe aux gueux* (beggar's weed), because beggars hoping for generous handouts would use it to irritate their skins and simulate sores. It is the basis of a homoeopathic remedy for skin eruptions.

TO KEEP HYDRANGEAS PINK, SPRINKLE THE SOIL WITH LIME

Pink is the natural colour of hydrangeas, but to keep them that way you need to make sure the soil stays alkaline – which is why lime does the trick. If you want blue hydrangeas, you should bury rusty nails under each plant.

Hydrangea flowers – nicknamed 'changeables' by the Victorians – are nature's soil indicators, but are the opposite of litmus paper. On acid soils the blooms will be blue, but you can turn them blue artificially by adding aluminium sulphate to the soil or watering with a blueing agent. Rusty nails or copper wire planted near the roots are effective old-fashioned blueing treatments.

The flowers on a hydrangea head are of two kinds: the small fertile flowers and the showy sterile flowers, the ray florets. The mop-headed hortensias and the flat-headed lacecaps of *Hydrangea macrophylla* are the best known, but *H. paniculata* 'Grandiflora' is a hardier choice in cold areas. For a more unusual look, search out *H. aspera*, with large velvety leaves and heads of fertile flowers bordered by just a few ray florets. Hydrangeas are native to Asia and the Americas and were probably introduced to Europe from Japan.

Hydrangeas get their name from the shape of their seedpods, which look like drinking cups. In Greek hydor *means 'water' and* angeion *'vessel'.*

FORSYTHIA IS THE SUNSHINE BUSH

An apt name for the shrub whose vivid yellow flowers herald the spring, and a hint at its cultural preferences. Loved and loathed in equal proportions, it is regarded either as a joy or a tired suburban cliché.

Forsythia makes its splash by producing its masses of blooms – borne on the previous year's wood – before the leaves appear. Choice of species is best dictated by the place in which you plan to grow it. Most will tolerate partial shade, though all prefer well drained soil. The pretty, arching *Forsythia suspensa* (which is excellent trained against a wall) and popular hybrids such as 'Beatrix Farrand' will grow to at least 1.8m (6ft), while *F. x intermedia* is more compact. Whichever you choose, prune it back hard as soon as it has flowered. If you cut it back in autumn you will have no flowers the following year.

PROS AND CONS

Extolling forsythia's virtues in 1901, the American garden writer Alice Morse Earle said: 'Forsythia shines out a grateful delight to the eyes and heart, concentrating for a week all the golden radiance of sunlight, which later will be shared by sister shrubs and flowers. *Forsythia suspensa*, falling in long sweeps of yellow bells, is in some favourable places a cascade of liquid light.'

A BRIGHT SPRING

Bring sunshine yellow into the spring garden with other attractive shrubs.
- Mahonia spp. *(Oregon grape) – architectural shrubs with prickly leaves and sprays of bright yellow bell-shaped, fragrant flowers.*
- Berberis buxifolia *(barberry) – orange-yellow flowers on an evergreen shrub armed with sharp spines.*
- Corylopsis pauciflora *– dense clusters of pale yellow flowers and bright green leaves that have a pink flush when they first appear.*
- Ribes odoratum *(buffalo currant) – small slightly drooping sprays of bright yellow flowers with a spicy scent similar to other flowering currants.*

Not every gardener has been so enamoured with forsythia. In his *Gardening Heresies and Devotions* of 1939 William Bowyer Honey expressed the view that it is fit only for outlying places in the wild garden, 'where at flowering time the colour and form of their bells can be enjoyed and their later bedragglement forgotten'.

IF IT LOOKS DIFFERENT, CUT IT OUT

Good advice for variegated shrubs, which often produce vigorous, plain-leaved branches. The same can happen to yellow-leaved shrubs such as varieties of philadelphus.

Plant leaves are green because they contain the pigment chlorophyll, vital for helping to convert energy from sunlight into food for the plant. In a variegated leaf, the pale areas contain little or no chlorophyll, and this tends to make them grow more slowly. When leaves are prettily variegated in pink or purple the chlorophyll is replaced by pigments known as anthocyanins.

Writing in 1895, Canon Henry Ellacombe extolled the virtues of variegated plants, claiming for them 'a special value in the winter decoration of our gardens'. Among his favourites were the variegated hollies, which 'brighten up a lawn in a wonderful way'. He identified his favourite as the milkmaid holly, available today as *Ilex aquifolium* 'Silver Milkmaid'.

MORE TIPS FOR SHRUB CARE
- *Prepare the soil well before you plant – and make sure the hole is big enough.*
- *If a shrub is not thriving, cut it back hard in spring. Feed well with a compost mulch and keep well watered.*
- *Look out for the red spots of coral spot disease and cut off any affected branches immediately.*
- *Transplant shrubs in winter when they are not actively growing.*
- *As a rule, the strongest shoots need the least pruning.*

Put roses wherever they will grow

A fitting tribute to the indubitable stars of the garden and their versatility. As befits their beauty, roses are symbols of perfection and womanhood, while the places where roses bloom are considered to be especially blessed.

Though traditionally grown in formal beds, roses work well in mixed beds, too, and contrast superbly with herbaceous perennials of all kinds. For a cottage garden effect mix them with phloxes, poppies and foxgloves, and underplant with violets and alchemillas. Roses mix wonderfully with lavender, and planting them with this, or with other strong-smelling herbs such as fennel, chives, tarragon and thyme, can help to deter aphids.

The delights of the rose garden have been enjoyed since ancient times, and a garland of roses has even been uncovered in an Egyptian tomb. Roses are depicted on the walls of the Minoan Palace of Knossos, in Crete, built around 1600 BC. They were classical symbols of love and beauty, and the Roman naturalist Pliny, writing in about AD 70, described roses growing 'everywhere in profusion'.

PLANTING AND PROPAGATING

As a rule, roses love the sun, so choose a sunny spot but make sure that the soil is well enriched with organic matter to provide food and conserve as much moisture as possible. Though roses are reputed to love clay soils – especially those in and around London – they hate to be waterlogged, so clay is best broken up with additions of lime and grit, or even with shredded newspapers.

KNOW YOUR ROSES

It helps greatly to know how to interpret the labels on roses. Select your roses from these main groups:

Species roses – vigorous descendants of wild roses, with long arching shoots and single flowers.

Old roses – the oldest rose hybrids, mostly double flowered, including the Gallica and Damask roses.

Hybrid teas – also known as large-flowered bush roses. Typically, flowers are about 10cm (4in) in diameter with high, conical centres and outer petals that curve back as they open.

Floribundas – also known as cluster-flowered bush roses, these are similar to hybrid teas but with smaller flowers in clusters of up to 20 blooms. Dwarf varieties are called patio roses.

Modern shrub roses – bred for their abundance of flowers and good disease resistance, in a wide variety of forms.

Climbers – repeat-flowering plants that send out long shoots and small clusters of blooms.

Ramblers – roses that flower only once a year, with more flexible shoots than true climbers.

Miniature roses – plants with twiggy shoots and tiny leaves much smaller than those of patio roses.

Ground-cover roses – low-growing, spreading roses, branching very freely and often repeat flowering.

Autumn is the ideal time to plant, but if you are buying bare-rooted roses wait until the weather is cold and the plants have become completely dormant. Soak the roots in water overnight before you begin to plant. If you buy container-grown roses, plant them while the soil is still warm, and water the plants well beforehand.

Roses are easy to propagate from cuttings taken in autumn, and there is an old country trick that can help boost your success rate. With a sharp knife, cut a cross in the base of the stem and insert a grain of wheat into the slit. Tie the base with raffia, then put the cutting in water and leave it to soak overnight. Pot up the cutting next day and leave it undisturbed until the spring in a cold frame or a sheltered spot in the garden.

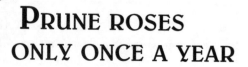

PRUNE ROSES ONLY ONCE A YEAR

The credo of some experts, who recommend only spring pruning, though cutting back in both autumn and spring is perfectly satisfactory for many roses. In winter it is also worth sawing away dead wood from the base of a rose, where diseases can take hold.

Between the end of winter and early spring is the perfect time to prune a rose, and even if new growth has started to appear in autumn this should be cut back too, to encourage really strong growth the following year.

First, cut away any dead, diseased or decayed wood. A good tip is to notice the colour of the wood as you cut. If it is brown, make more cuts until you reach paler, live wood. Another general rule is to open up the centre of the plant as much as possible.

Be bold with your rose pruning when you need to. After planting a hybrid tea (large-flowered) rose, or to rejuvenate a tired specimen, cut it down to about 15cm (6in) above the base. For floribundas (cluster-flowered) types, take the growth down to around 25cm (9in). Try to make angled cuts just above a bud facing in the direction in which you would like the new shoot to grow.

You don't always need the secateurs. Vigorous large and cluster-flowered roses will respond well to an autumn cut with shears. You can then repeat the operation in spring.

THE RULES FOR CLIMBERS AND RAMBLERS

For climbers, you should reduce shoots on which flowers have been borne to three or four buds every year. For rambling roses, aim to cut about a third of the old growth to ground level once a year, then train vigorous new shoots coming from the base of the plant by tying them in to the support.

Lavender blooms for our taking

Meaning that the flowers, once picked, have many uses. One of the most useful garden plants, the scent and form of lavender – and the bees and butterflies it attracts – are superb for months on end.

Hardiest and most reliable of all the lavenders is the old English *Lavandula angustifolia* and its varieties, such as the compact variety 'Hidcote', with deep purple flowers, and the white-flowered 'Alba'. More tender are the French lavenders (*L. stoechas*), which are especially vulnerable to having their roots exposed to cold and damp over the winter, though the butterfly lavender 'Papillon' is worth pampering as it is always a delight.

To keep lavenders flowering well they need a light trim in autumn, but don't cut into the old wood. If a plant has become very straggly cut it hard back in the spring, before new growth starts to sprout. To protect favourite, less hardy lavenders from winter frost, a practical – but not particularly attractive – solution is to drape some fleece over them.

Essential oil

It is one of the joys of travelling in southern Europe – and in Norfolk in England – to see fields of lavender in flower in the summer. Originally these would largely have been wild or semi-wild expanses, like those described by John Parkinson when writing about the production of lavender oil in the Mediterranean region in the 17th century: 'Lavender groweth in Spain abundantly, in many places so wilde, and little regarded, that many have gone, and abiden there to distill the oyle thereof, whereof great quantity now cometh over from thence unto us; and also in Languedock, and Provence in France.'

The essential oil of lavender has an antiseptic effect, and has many uses. It can be put on bites, stings and spots; it soothes burns, and was traditionally brushed on bedsteads to rid them of bedbugs, and on the heads of children to kill head lice and nits. Lavender water was used to bathe the temples to calm pain and fever; for insomnia and digestive problems, an infusion of lavender flowers was recommended.

Lavender also has its uses in the kitchen. Savoury aspic jelly was once flavoured with lavender and both the leaves and flowers of L. *angustifolia* can be used in salads and salad dressings, ice creams and sweet drinks. Crystallized in sugar, lavender flowers make a pretty, edible decoration for cakes and biscuits.

LAVENDER'S BLUE

There are many different versions of the nursery rhyme that features lavender. The best known begins 'Lavender's blue, diddle diddle, /Lavender's green', but the oldest one, dating to the mid-17th century and entitled 'Diddle Diddle, or, The Kind Country Lovers', begins:

Lavender's green, diddle diddle,
Lavender's blue,
You must love me, diddle diddle,
cause I love you,
I heard one say, diddle diddle,
since I came hither,
That you and I, diddle diddle,
must lie together.

The plant's name may derive ultimately from the Latin lavare, *meaning 'to wash', from which came the Old French* lavanderie, *a laundry. Washing draped over the bushes was delicately scented as it dried in the sunshine.*

STRIKE HARDWOOD CUTTINGS WITHOUT LEAVES

A tried and tested way of increasing woody plants and, when it works, extremely satisfying as well as money saving. The trick is to get the cuttings to take root, which even the most experienced gardeners can find hit and miss.

Hardwood cuttings are best taken between mid-autumn and early spring. Take the cutting as close as possible to the stem of the parent plant so as not to leave a 'snag' on the end. Take off the leaves, being sure to remember which is the top, and, if you wish, dip the trimmed 'root' end in hormone rooting powder, tapping it lightly afterwards to remove any excess powder. Insert the cutting in soil or compost to about a third of its length.

The cuttings of some plants, such as rhododendrons, strike best if you make an upward slit about 12mm (½in) long in the base.

Cuttings of roses, buddleia, rosemary and jasmine, which root relatively easily, can be put straight into a garden bed in a relatively sheltered spot that does not dry out. Otherwise pot cuttings in a mixture of compost and add sharp sand to act as a stimulant. By the following autumn they should have rooted and be ready to plant or pot on.

Gardeners of old would keep their cuttings under a bell jar to conserve warmth and guarantee high humidity. A cold frame is a good substitute, or even a thick plastic bag.

Vita Sackville-West recommended growing a forsythia hedge entirely from cuttings rooted directly into the soil. For, she said, 'I never believe in moving plants if one can possibly help it.'

PRUNE SHRUBS AFTER FLOWERING

This is fine for shrubs that flower early in the year, but not sensible for those that bloom later. The key to success is knowing which type of branches bear flowers.

Pruning is one of the most satisfying of garden jobs, and all but the slowest-growing shrubs need pruning to keep them in shape and promote flowering. A yearly cut will make them strong and bushy. As for timing, use these four basic rules:

1. Shrubs that flower on new wood, relatively late in the season, such as ceanothus, hydrangeas, spiraeas and buddleia, need pruning early in the year.
2. Shrubs that flower on wood made the year before, such as forsythia, winter jasmine and early weigelas, should be pruned immediately after flowering.
3. Shrubs that flower on old wood can be cut back at any time after flowering, but for preference in early spring. Cistus, cotoneaster and hibiscus come into this category.
4. Shrubs that flower in summer on wood of the previous year can be cut back after flowering – if they need it. Plants in this category include lilacs, flowering currants and philadelphus.

Among his armoury of tools the Victorian gardener would have a pruning saw for larger branches, and for pruning shrubs he would favour shears looking rather like small, squat secateurs, but with blades of equal size.

THE ART OF TOPIARY OFFERS MUCH TO ADMIRE

If it is to your taste. With proper attention to scale and position, a topiary shrub or hedge can make an outstanding garden feature. This ancient art has been beloved since Roman times.

The Roman naturalist Pliny was one of the first to describe topiary – cypress trees cut into the shape of hunting scenes, sailing ships and 'all sorts of images'. Tudor gardens such as Hampton Court near London boasted topiary chequerboards but also 'all manner of shapes, men and women, half men and half horse, sirens, serving maids with baskets, French lilies and delicate crenellations all round'.

Topiary reached the height of complexity in the formal Renaissance gardens of Versailles, designed by André Le Nôtre (1613–1700), and other grand gardens of 17th- and 18th-century France, which also sported superb fountains and sculptures. In 1745, to celebrate his son's wedding, Louis XV held the Ball of the Clipped Yew Trees, which he himself attended in fancy dress – as a clipped yew.

Many evergreens are suitable subjects for topiary, but cypress, box and yew, which have small leaves and do not grow too quickly, remain the most popular choices with good reason. Classically, cones, blocks and pyramids were the preferred shapes, but today anything goes, from renditions of animals and birds to soft, informal cloud-like designs. Start with a simple shape and clip with small sheep shears for a close, neat finish. Feed the plants with a slow-release fertilizer to help ensure even growth.

'I, for my part, do not like Images cut out in Juniper or other Garden Stuff; they be for children.'
Francis Bacon,
Of Gardens, 1597

GROW ROSEMARY FOR REMEMBRANCE

A saying dating back to the ancient Greeks that was immortalized by Ophelia in Shakespeare's *Hamlet*. A cook's staple, rosemary is easy to grow as long as it has plenty of sunshine and well-drained soil.

For the ancients, rosemary symbolized not only remembrance but also fidelity and friendship. It was woven into funeral wreaths and added to wedding bouquets. Greek students even wore rosemary garlands in their hair to enhance their performance in examinations.

For the gardener, rosemary (*Rosmarinus officinalis*) is a useful aromatic shrub. Although most varieties have blue or purple flowers, white-flowered varieties such as *R. albiflorus* are well worth looking for. For ground cover,

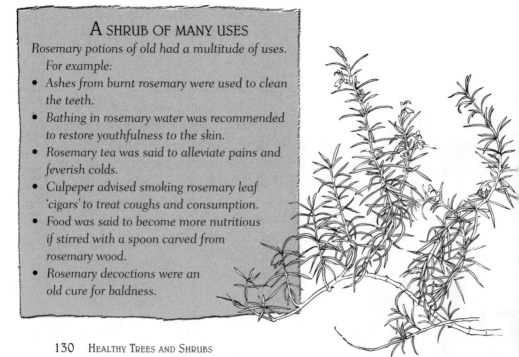

A SHRUB OF MANY USES

Rosemary potions of old had a multitude of uses. For example:

- *Ashes from burnt rosemary were used to clean the teeth.*
- *Bathing in rosemary water was recommended to restore youthfulness to the skin.*
- *Rosemary tea was said to alleviate pains and feverish colds.*
- *Culpeper advised smoking rosemary leaf 'cigars' to treat coughs and consumption.*
- *Food was said to become more nutritious if stirred with a spoon carved from rosemary wood.*
- *Rosemary decoctions were an old cure for baldness.*

varieties such as 'Jackman's Prostrate', which rarely reach more than 30cm (1ft), are ideal. The biggest problem with rosemary is that, being of Mediterranean origin, it can be prone to frost damage and may need winter protection in cold areas or frost pockets.

BOX BREATHES THE FRAGRANCE OF ETERNITY

An observation based on a quote from the American author and poet Oliver Wendell Holmes, who was a supreme observer of both gardens and the natural world. Box, used for centuries in the garden, has a unique odour.

In his romance *Elsie Venner*, written in 1861, Holmes describes how a couple '… walked over the crackling leaves in the garden, between the lines of Box, breathing its fragrance of eternity; for this is one of the odors which carry us out of time into the abysses of the unbeginning past; if we ever lived on another ball of stone than this, it must be that there was Box growing on it.'

The Romans loved box for its neat shape when clipped (see page 129) and box hedging was an outstanding feature of the gardens of Fishbourne Palace in Sussex, a villa built towards the end of the first century AD. It has remained popular, though not all gardeners relish its distinctive scent.

Box is easy to grow and long lived. It needs plenty of water when young, but grows quickly and develops useful drought tolerance. To ensure uniformity of size, shape and leaf colour it is best to buy young plants from a nursery or to raise your own from cuttings. As well as the common box (*Buxus sempervirens*), which comes in plain and variegated varieties, for a really miniature hedge *B. microphylla* is probably a better choice.

Queen Anne so disliked the box hedges at Hampton Court that she had them all destroyed. Many garden owners followed suit and uprooted their hedges.

5. FIGHTING WEEDS, PESTS AND DISEASES

Since a garden is, by its very essence, 'nature tamed', it is no surprise that gardeners feel themselves to be constantly at odds with the forces of the natural world. Even in the depths of winter it seems that no garden is ever free of weeds, pests or diseases, though modern ways of treating them, particularly organic methods, are considerably more benign than in times past. The Victorian gardener employed a whole laboratory of dangerous chemicals to kill unwelcome intruders, and only recently has the list of acceptable treatments been revised to eliminate some systemic formulas that may endanger human health.

Weeds may be most unwelcome in the vegetable patch and decorative border, but they have their place in the wild garden, where they encourage butterflies, bees and other welcome creatures. And it is worth remembering that in the monastery gardens of the Middle Ages there were no such things as weeds because – like dandelions and nettles – every plant had its uses, either in the kitchen or in the medicine chest.

It may be a war out there, but there are few things in life more satisfying than the contemplation of a weed-free garden or the enjoyment of perfect fruit and vegetables free of disease. You need only remember the old adage that 'the good vineyard does not require prayers, but a hoe'.

Hoe, hoe, hoe

Weeds need to be kept at bay because, as any gardener knows, they are always growing. An hour's concentrated weeding can be hugely therapeutic, and hoes, which come in a variety of designs, are also useful for other garden jobs.

The Spanish hoe, which became known as 'Lord Vernon's new tillage hoe' in 19th-century English gardening manuals, has a pointed blade and can be useful for creating shallow seed drills as well as for weeding and 'stirring the ground among small articles'.

For getting rid of annual weeds with shallow roots before they can seed or overwhelm crops and flowers, the best hoe is the Dutch or thrust hoe, which, as its name implies, is used by pushing it away from the body. The advantage of this type, as Robert Thompson observed in his classic Victorian guide *The Gardener's Assistant*, is that 'it can be used to a considerable extent without going out of the alleys [gaps between rows], so that the ground is not trodden on.'

On stiff, lumpy ground, a draw hoe, which is pulled towards the body, may be more effective. This is probably the oldest hoe design, made in Mesopotamia around 4000 BC with a wooden handle and a flint head. Though it is now fitted with a long handle, until the 19th century the draw hoe was popularly short handled, and was used in a kneeling position.

The right technique

Arm action is all-important for effective hoeing, as perfectly described by Charles Dudley Warner, writing in 1876: there should be a 'broad, free sweep of the instrument, which kills the weeds, spares the plants, and loosens the soil without leaving holes and hills'. And ideally, hoeing should be done every couple of days, especially in spring when the rate of weed growth is at its peak.

For some jobs a special hoe is best. For weeding onions and other rows of vegetables the onion hoe is ideal. Swan-necked and short-handled, its blade is no more than 5cm (2in) wide.

BURN FOR HYGIENE

By far the best way to get rid of diseased plant material.
A bonfire may be a pleasurable experience for you, but
perhaps not for your neighbours. Because bonfire smoke can
easily be a cause of aggravation, it is best to take care – and
be mindful of the wind – before you burn.

As well as diseased plant material of all kinds, perennial weeds and tree prunings are excellent candidates for the bonfire, though nothing will burn well unless it is thoroughly dry. While a good breeze will help to oxygenate the fire and make it flare brightly, it will also blow smoke around, hence the need for prudence.

Save the ash from your fire and put it on your roses or raspberries as an excellent fertilizer.

Your fire will create least smoke when it is really hot. To get it burning well, a corrugated iron 'wind tunnel' set against it, in the direction of the prevailing wind, can speed the heating process. However, bonfires can be notoriously slow to get going, and firelighters may be the best solution. Never, ever, douse the fire with paraffin.

In Britain, it is the custom to save garden wood and other rubbish to burn on Bonfire Night, 5 November, in memory of Guy Fawkes, who was hanged for his part in the Gunpowder Plot of 1605 to blow up the Houses of Parliament. A stuffed effigy of Guy Fawkes traditionally tops the bonfire.

Now is the time for the burning of the leaves.
They go to the fire; the nostril pricks with smoke
Wandering slowly into the weeping mist.
Brittle and blotched, ragged and rotten sheaves!

(Laurence Binyon, 'The Burning of the Leaves', 1944)

WATER BEFORE YOU WEED

It's much easier to get weeds out of damp soil, though rain is the best watering of all. Fortunately, however, weeds grow less strongly in dry spells.

Effective hand weeding – especially when dealing with the nastiest perennials, such as convolvulus and creeping thistles – depends on getting all the roots out, or at least as much of the root as possible. You need to be able to dig deep, which is more difficult when the soil is dry and hard. If, however, you use a chemical alternative such as glyphosate, the leaves of your enemy plants need to be really dry, so watering is not recommended.

Ideally, pick a fine spell and use weedkiller on strongly growing plants. A good tip for convolvulus is to train it up separate sticks so that you can spray the winding stems individually or paint the glyphosate on the leaves. Be careful to shield any prized plants nearby.

IF YOUR WEEDS ARE NETTLES, YOUR SOIL IS RICH IN NITROGEN

Nettles have long been used to make an iron-rich tea, but they should be picked before May Day. After that, so legend has it, the Devil uses them to make his shirts.

True. Many other weeds are also excellent indicators of your soil type, the improvement it needs and the plants that will thrive.

Since nettles mean nitrogen, they are a sign that your plot will be ideal for leafy vegetables such as spinach, but may be less suitable for fruit trees, which will make too much leaf and too little fruit. To balance up the soil, treat it with potash, which, on soil already rich in nitrogen, is best supplied as potassium sulphate.

Phosphorus is the other essential element, ensuring good root and fruit formation. It is best given to the soil as phosphates, either in quick-acting liquid form or as slow-release rock phosphate. Good organic sources are farmyard manure and bone meal.

BENEFITS OF NETTLES

To attract butterflies and moths, leave a patch of nettles growing in a wild area of your garden. The beautiful burnished brass moth (*Diachrysia chrysitis*) and the small tortoiseshell butterfly (*Aglais urticae*) lay their eggs on nettle leaves, which are subsequently avidly devoured by the caterpillars.

Nettles make an excellent rose fertilizer. If the plants are gathered and soaked in water for a month, using 10 litres (17½ pints) of water for every 1kg (2lb 3oz) of nettles, the resulting liquid can be watered directly on to the soil at the plants' roots.

HELPFUL SIGNS
Look out for all these good soil indicators growing in your garden:
High nitrogen – stinging nettles (*Urtica dioica*), black nightshade (*Solanum nigrum*)
Lime rich – bindweed (*Convolvulus arvensis*)
Lime deficient – chamomile (*Chamaemelum nobile*)
Loam – tansy (*Tanacetum vulgare*), dandelions (*Taraxacum* spp)
Clay – coltsfoot (*Tussilago farfara*)

TOO MUCH WATER WELCOMES DISEASE

Overwatering – especially of cuttings and seedlings – is a sure way to encourage the growth of the agents of rot and mould, which can kill in a matter of hours.

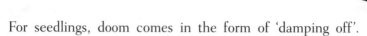

For seedlings, doom comes in the form of 'damping off'. A fungus of the genus *Pythium* or *Phythophthora* attacks them, making them keel over. In many seedlings it is the stems just above soil level that are infected, but in cucumber seedlings the roots are most vulnerable. Too much water encourages these fungi to thrive, as do over-cool conditions, overcrowding and using unsterilized compost.

Cuttings will also become infected and perish when overwatered. While they should never be allowed to dry out completely, sparing applications of water are better than too much. If you are growing cuttings in pots outdoors, avoid setting the pots in saucers where water can accumulate.

EARLY WATERING SYSTEM

The first cans with spouts appeared in the 17th century. The original watering cans, made in the fifth century, were clay pots with perforated bases. Writing in 1577, Thomas Hill described the water pot and the way it was used: 'The common watering pot for the Garden beds with us, hath a narrow neck, big belly, somewhat large bottom, and full of little holes, with a proper hole formed on the head to take in the water, which filled full, and the thumb laid on the hole to keep in the aire, may in such wise be carried in handsome manner to those places by a better help aiding, in the turning and bearing upright of the bottom of this pot, which needfully require watering.'

> A old way of preventing damping off is to water seedlings little and often with cold chamomile tea.

ONLY NETTING WILL KEEP RABBITS AWAY

This is a fine and humane solution for a vegetable garden, as long as it is dug in deeply enough, but it is hardly aesthetic perfection for a herbaceous border that is under attack.

The rabbit's love of garden crops is perfectly captured in Beatrix Potter's *The Tale of Peter Rabbit*: 'First he ate some lettuces and some French beans; and then he ate some radishes; and then, feeling rather sick, he went to look for some parsley.' Rabbits will ravage young foliage of all kinds, though they are less keen on strong-tasting vegetables such as leeks and onions.

Hungry rabbits can leap 60cm (2ft) and more, and burrow at least 30cm (1ft) below ground, which means that fencing should be of 2.5cm (1in) mesh, 1m (3ft) high and sunk at least 50cm (18in) into the ground. To stop it sagging, stout posts at 1.5m (4½ft) intervals are recommended.

RABBIT PLAGUE

As well as shooting them, farmers have traditionally hunted rabbits by releasing ferrets into their warrens, but a more drastic step was taken with the deliberate introduction of infection. First tested in Australia in 1938, the *Myxoma* virus was released there in 1950 with devastating effect: it reduced the estimated rabbit population from 600 million to 100 million in just two years. Myxomatosis reached Britain – probably from France – in 1953. Since then, natural resistance has built up, but it is still possible to see a rabbit with the ghastly puffed-up head and infected eyes typical of 'mixie'.

On the Isle of Portland in Dorset the rabbit is considered so unlucky that its name is never spoken. Portland quarrymen will turn back home from the journey to work should a rabbit cross their path.

Pick off caterpillars by hand

And the eggs, too, if you have the patience and the stomach for this rather disgusting job. Your efforts will pay off handsomely, keeping the leaves of your vegetables from being eaten to skeletons.

The word 'caterpillar', first recorded in the 15th century, may come from the French for 'old foraging cat'. Old country names include 'snortywinks' and 'nanny-viper'.

The caterpillars that do most damage in the vegetable garden are those that hatch from eggs laid in groups (usually on the undersides of leaves) by cabbage white butterflies. These are in fact, two distinct species, the large white (*Pieris brassicae*) and the small white (*P. rapae*). As well as size, an easy way to distinguish the two is by the black wingtips on the former and grey wingtips on the latter.

The caterpillars of both butterflies munch with equal fervour on brassicas such as cabbages, broccoli and

Brussels sprouts in the intense feeding stage of their life cycle. Large white caterpillars are predominantly bright yellow with black markings, while small white caterpillars are green with yellow markings.

KEEP DEER OUT OF YOUR GARDEN WITH SOAP

This old-fashioned remedy is very unlikely to be effective, even if you choose the strongest carbolic. Although there are other smell-based remedies, only judicious choice of plants – and effective fencing – will keep your garden free from the ravages of deer.

A hungry deer can eat as much as 4.5kg (10lb) of vegetation a day. And deer do not clip plants neatly. Because they have no upper front teeth they pull or tear plants apart. Deer tastes vary with the season. In spring they favour tender grass and herbaceous greenery, in summer they will feed on roses, petunias or even tomatoes, and in winter they will eat the shoots and bark of woody shrubs and trees. They have even been known to stand on their hind legs and take the nuts from garden bird feeders.

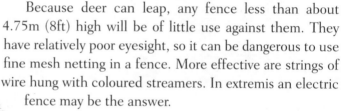

Because deer can leap, any fence less than about 4.75m (8ft) high will be of little use against them. They have relatively poor eyesight, so it can be dangerous to use fine mesh netting in a fence. More effective are strings of wire hung with coloured streamers. In extremis an electric fence may be the answer.

Of all the odours likely to keep deer at bay, that of coyote urine is believed to be best, though the evidence for its effectiveness is all anecdotal. It is usually sold mixed with hot pepper wax and dispensed in the form of small plastic darts. The smell and bark of a domestic dog can also work well as a deterrent.

Deer have been renowned throughout history for their gentleness and sensitivity. They have been observed to shed tears when pursued, but these are, in fact, oily secretions produced by the frightened animals.

DEER-PROOF SELECTIONS

Some plants are less to the liking of deer, though in cold weather they will eat almost anything. Most are effective because deer dislike their smell or taste, or because they are spiky.

Annuals – *pot marigolds, zinnias, lupins, Canterbury bells, busy lizzies, forget-me-nots*

Perennials – *agave, monkshood, bamboo, shasta daisy, hellebore, narcissus, penstemon, foxglove, potato vine, periwinkle*

Shrubs – *berberis, buddleia, box, ceanothus, daphne, cotoneaster, holly, juniper, sage, jasmine*

Trees – *yew, spruce, bottlebrush, ash, eucalyptus, cordyline*

Deter slugs and snails with gravel

Every gardener has a favourite method of dealing with slugs and snails – from the chemical blast of pellets to wildlife-friendly methods such as surrounding plants with sharp gravel to impede the creatures' progress.

Since slugs can ravage beautiful young hostas, delphiniums or clematis overnight, not to mention destroying salad plants and even climbing up raspberry canes to gorge on ripe fruit, it is hardly surprising that gardeners loathe them with a passion. Some people swear that the only way to get rid of them is to go out into the garden at night and pick them individually off paths, beds and plants. They can then be drowned in a bucket of soapy water.

Slugs and snails are molluscs whose bodies consist largely of a muscular foot (which in snails curls up inside the shell). This not only secretes their tell-tale lubricating silvery trails, but contains organs of touch and smell powerful enough to detect potential food from a distance. Once a tasty meal has been located they munch through it using sharp file-like oral rasps. In a season a single slug is believed to be able to eat up to 800g (1lb 12oz) of plant material. They are also prolific breeders, producing as many as a hundred eggs each, per year.

In recent times gardeners have marked snail shells with a dab of paint, taken them some distance away and discovered that they will actually 'home'.

Slug-proof choices

Many suppliers advertise hostas bred to have some resistance to slugs. They have names like 'Big Daddy', 'Invincible' and 'Great Expectations', but they are unlikely to be able to stave off attacks completely. However, slugs really don't like the furry foliage of plants such as stachys and are deterred by the strong smells of mint, geraniums, foxgloves, fennel, and all the members of the onion family, especially garlic (see below). Or you can plant some 'sacrificial' comfrey, which is a real slug magnet.

Because, as granny extolled, prevention is better than cure, good gardening practice can help keep slugs at bay and minimize the damage. Regular hoeing will bring their eggs to the surface, where they will provide food for birds, while clearing away decaying matter will deprive slugs of their breeding grounds. Remember, too, that the stronger the plant the more likely it is to be able to resist attack from slugs.

ORGANIC METHODS OF SLUG CONTROL

Gravel and glass chippings – *uncomfortable and difficult for slugs to negotiate.*

Diatomaceous earth – *the fine powder absorbs moisture from the creatures, causing them to die from dehydration.*

Beer traps – *the smell is irresistible and death is by drowning.*

Copper rings – *offensive to the taste buds on slugs' bodies.*

Dilute cat urine – *interferes with body chemistry.*

Coffee grounds – *fatal caffeine poisoning.*

Crushed garlic – *probably damages the nervous system.*

Salt – *destroys slug metabolism by dehydration.*

Frogs, toads and hedgehogs – *dine on slugs and snails.*

Upturned grapefruit halves with holes cut in them – *the animals glide in then can't escape.*

Nematodes – *parasitic worms infest and kill slugs and snails.*

A 'slugabed' is an Old English word for a lazy lie-abed. But a 'slughorn' is a battle trumpet.

SCARE BIRDS AWAY WITH THEIR OWN FEATHERS

Erecting a potato stuck with feathers on a stick is an old way of keeping away birds – a basic form of scarecrow. If only preventing bird attacks were so simple! You can try everything from making a bird kite to hanging up shiny CDs, but in the end you may have to resort to netting.

The bird kite is made in the silhouette of a bird of prey, such as a hawk, and tied on a long string so that it hovers above the plot. This is fine as long as it is windy enough to keep the scarer aloft and, as with other deterrents, birds quickly grow wise to it. The scarecrow, which can become equally familiar, has been standing in fields since time immemorial, though the first written account dates from the 16th century. The farmer would use his old clothes to dress his creation, which might be attached to a baker's peel, the pole used to move loaves in and out of the oven. Standing with his arms outstretched, as on a crucifix, gives the scarecrow the look and feel of a human sacrifice.

The *Household Cyclopedia* of 1881 was certain that a scarecrow is of no use unless combined with a loud bang: 'The most effectual method of banishing them [crows] from a field, as far as experience goes, is to combine with one or another of the scarecrows in vogue the frequent use of the musket. Nothing strikes such terror into these sagacious animals as the sight of a fowling-piece and the explosion of gunpowder, which they have known so often to be fatal to their race.'

In Britain the scarecrow is known by various names: in Somerset he is a mommet and in Devon a murmet. In the Isle of Wight he is a hodmedod and in East Anglia a mawhini. When placed in potato fields, scarecrows are tattie bogies or bouies.

USE A CARROT TRAP TO EXTERMINATE WIREWORMS

One of various ways to attract wireworms, grubs that can ruin an entire crop by boring into stems, roots and tubers. These avid tunnellers are the larvae of the click beetle, which lays its eggs in early summer, usually among weeds.

Wireworms can attack carrots, turnips, beetroot, celery, onions and lettuce, but potatoes are most susceptible of all. When lifting the crop, the wireworms – which are shiny and orange, with stiff bodies up to 25mm (1in) long – can be seen protruding from holes in the potato tubers, making them at best unfit for storing and, at worst, inedible.

Carrot traps are simply pieces of carrot (or potato) pushed into sticks and buried about 5–10cm (2–4in) below the surface, from the time potato tubers start to swell. Every couple of weeks, pull up the traps and dispose of the wireworms that have been attracted to them.

If wireworms are a problem in your vegetable patch it is wise to harvest potatoes as soon as they are mature, rather than leaving them in the ground. Because wireworms are able to live in the soil for four years or more before metamorphosing into adults, another good ruse is to sow a crop of green manure, such as mustard, in late summer, next to your potatoes. This will not only attract the wireworms away from the potatoes but will give them sufficient food to speed up their maturation.

The click beetle (*Agriotes* sp) is named for its snapping sound. When turned on its back it arches its body upwards, then suddenly straightens up, making a spine on its underside slide into a groove with a loud click. This sends the beetle spinning through the air.

DRESS TREE WOUNDS FOR HEALTH

A way to protect the wood of a damaged or severely pruned tree from invasion by organisms that can damage or even kill it, but not universally recommended. Good pruning technique will help keep the risk of disease to a minimum.

Trees usually need pruning to improve their shape, stimulate growth and keep their size within reasonable bounds. But, as the garden writer W.H. Rowe pointed out, 'Whereas the judicious use of the knife or saw is an important and necessary part of tree and shrub cultivation, the reckless employment of these implements can wreak havoc.'

When taking off a branch you need to ensure a clean cut. To do this – and to prevent the branch breaking off and ripping away part of the tree trunk – you need to begin from the underside, cutting about two-thirds of the way through the branch. You can then complete the cut from above. Advice of old recommended keeping the cut as close to the trunk as possible, but new research suggests that this risks removing the 'collar' – the swollen area at the base of a branch that sometimes has a ridge of bark on it. The importance of this collar is that it contains a chemical zone that inhibits the spread of decay in the trunk, so removing it during pruning greatly increases the chances of the trunk becoming infected by decay and canker-causing micro-organisms.

It is a similar story with wound dressings. The creosote used in the past, and even the shellac favoured today, are now believed to work contrary to the tree's natural healing process.

Cankers are swollen-edged cracks that appear on tree bark that has been killed. In the most serious cases, caused by the organism Phytophthora, they may also 'bleed'. In hot, dry weather, scraping away the outer bark in the early stages may allow the canker to dry up and the bark to heal, but little else can be done.

LADYBIRDS ARE THE GARDENERS' FRIENDS

The ladybird, ladybug or lady-cow is our ally because both the adults and their larvae, also known as 'garden crocodiles', are voracious devourers of aphids and scale insects.

Ladybirds (members of the insect family Coccinellidae) can eat up to 150 aphids in a day. The eggs, mostly laid on the undersides of leaves, hatch into elongated larvae, dark grey with coloured blotches, which consume many times their own weight in other insects before turning into the spherical pupae from which new adults hatch.

If you want more ladybirds in your garden it may be worth trying a 'ladybug lure', a product that incorporates a chemical attractant that simulates the scent of aphids, luring ladybirds, lacewings and other beneficial insects with the scent of their favourite food. You may also be able to buy ladybird larvae to increase your population.

As a ladybird flies from your hand it will fly in the direction of your true love if you say the rhyme: 'Ladybird, ladybird, fly away, flee! Tell me which way my wedding's to be.'

COUNT THE SPOTS

The most common European ladybird is the red seven-spot (*Coccinella 7-punctata*). The ladybird or 'beetle of our lady' got its name because its seven spots were taken to represent the joys and sorrows of the Virgin Mary. The rhyme 'Ladybird, ladybird fly away home/ Your house is on fire and your children will burn' is said to come from the burning of English hop fields at the end of the harvest, which destroyed many of these insects. As well as flying away when disturbed, ladybirds will lie on their backs and 'play possum'. To make themselves look unappetizing to bird predators they can also exude blobs of yellow 'blood'.

The Australian ladybird or vedalia beetle (*Rodolia cardinalis*) was taken to Pacific North America, where it successfully eradicated the cotton-cushion scale from orange and lemon orchards. The yellow *Thea 22-punctata* has 22 black spots, but the one with most spots is *Subcoccinella vigintiquattuorpunctata* or *S. 24-punctata* for short. You may also find 'aberrant' ladybirds with no spots at all. Less welcome is the harlequin ladybird (*Harmonia axyridis*), the most invasive ladybird on earth, named for its variable appearance. Introduced to North America from Asia in 1988, this 'grey squirrel of the insect world' arrived in Britain in summer 2004. Although an excellent aphid controller, when food is scarce it preys on native ladybirds and the eggs, larvae and caterpillars of other insects.

POLLEN BEETLES WILL FALL INTO YELLOW BUCKETS

… which you can fill with water to drown them, if you must. While they may mar the look of your prize blooms, these little round beetles are, as their name suggests, important garden pollinators.

Why a yellow bucket? Because pollen beetles (*Meligethes* spp.) are hugely attracted to the colour. When they first emerge in early spring, they head straight for daffodils and other yellow flowers. But yellow is not their only favourite. Sweet peas of any hue – but particularly pale colours – red runner bean flowers, dahlias and daisies are all effective lures for the beetles. In sweet peas they are particularly annoying because they lodge inside the flower keels (hoping, if female, to lay eggs there as well as feed).

If you pick infested flowers and bring them indoors, the beetles, which are black with a metallic,

Pollen grains are a plant's minute male germ cells, and every plant has its personal pollen design, as individual as a fingerprint. The study of buried pollen thousands of years old is used in studies from archaeology into the investigation of ancient climate change.

blue-green sheen, quickly emerge, flying towards the light. Again, a yellow bucket will come in handy. You may also want to put one under your washing line, as pollen beetles will head for yellow clothes hanging out to dry.

PLANT MARIGOLDS TO KEEP WHITEFLY AWAY

French marigolds (*Tagetes patula*) are the best of garden deterrents, though unlikely to be totally effective. They work best in a greenhouse to protect tomatoes and chrysanthemums, when planted tight up to your most vulnerable plants.

It is probably the musty odour of the flowers that deters whitefly, though their colour may also attract the pests away from crop plants. Playing to this colour preference, try hanging yellow sticky flypapers in the greenhouse or above plants growing outdoors. The insects, which look like tiny moths, will come to a permanent halt as they adhere to the trap. Another good organic control is the parasitic wasp *Encarsia formosa,* which works by laying its eggs in the whitefly larvae. The grubs that emerge from the eggs devour their hosts before they can hatch into adult flies.

Outdoors, plants most prone to whitefly are brassicas of all kinds, including cabbages, cauliflowers and broccoli. An infestation can be so bad that the leaves become covered with a sticky black substance and clouds of insects fly up when the plants are touched. The chemical controls that work best are malathion, sprayed regularly on the undersides of the leaves, or a systemic insecticide.

Despite their common name, French marigolds come from Mexico. Their name comes from the popular belief that they were introduced to Britain in 1572 by Huguenot refugees from France.

KILL DANDELIONS WITH SALT

This good old-fashioned organic technique works by interfering with the natural working of plant cells, or by preventing their growth, but it is not as effective as modern systemic treatments.

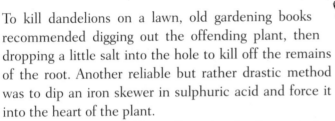

To kill dandelions on a lawn, old gardening books recommended digging out the offending plant, then dropping a little salt into the hole to kill off the remains of the root. Another reliable but rather drastic method was to dip an iron skewer in sulphuric acid and force it into the heart of the plant.

Modern weedkillers formulated for zapping perennial troublemakers such as dandelions contain chemicals such as glyphosate and are applied as 'spot' treatment on individual plants. For lawns, try a 'weed and feed' mixture, but be sure to apply it after rain, or when the lawn has been well watered, or it will scorch the grass.

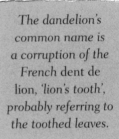

The dandelion's common name is a corruption of the French dent de lion, 'lion's tooth', probably referring to the toothed leaves.

WINTER SALADS

Young dandelion leaves can be eaten as salad greens. They have a slightly bitter taste not unlike that of chicory. In the past, gardeners were advised to lift the roots in the autumn, place them in boxes of soil and force the leaves into growth in a warm, dark place. Extracts of dandelion have long been used to treat urinary complaints and as a diuretic, to help produce urine – leading to its old nickname, 'piss a bed'.

PINCH OUT BROAD BEAN TOPS TO GET RID OF BLACK FLY

A good way of reducing the infestation, even it if fails to clear it completely. Another tip is to sow broad beans early – traditionally it was done on Boxing Day – so that they are well on the way to maturity before aphids appear in number.

Broad beans (*Vicia faba*), known in America as fava beans, can be successfully overwintered, although seed producers recommend sowing in late autumn while the soil is still warm. The earlier they are sown the less prone they will be to attack by aphids, which thrive on juicy, young plant growth and, if allowed to establish themselves, can literally make stems look pure black.

Gardeners can choose between two types: short-podded Windsor beans (probably the original ingredient of brown Windsor soup), with four large beans to a pod, and longpod varieties with up to eight beans per pod. As with peas, 19th-century gardeners would roll them in paraffin before planting to stop seeds being eaten by mice (see also page 155).

BEANS FRESH AND DRIED

For millennia, broad or field beans were the staple food of Europe, North Africa and Western Asia, and retained their popularity until American haricot beans (*Phaseolus vulgaris*) began to be imported to Europe in the 16th century. Picked young and tender, broad beans need little cooking and freeze beautifully.

Broad beans are a favourite food of squirrels – so be prepared to erect defensive barricades against these marauders.

When they are slightly larger many cooks prefer to serve them without their pale skins, which can be squeezed off between finger and thumb after cooking. The beans within are a wonderful bright green, a perfect accompaniment to ham or salmon, especially in a parsley sauce.

Large beans develop tough skins and are better dried, and it is these that are the key ingredient of the Egyptian national dish *ful medames*, one of the first cooked dishes ever recorded.

PLANT POTATOES TO CLEAR A PATCH OF WEEDS

A traditional way of clearing the ground that works particularly well with perennial weeds, though it is not totally effective against such horrors as bindweed – rightly nicknamed Devil's guts – or horsetails.

This method works because potatoes are regularly earthed up during their growing season, so that weeds are prevented from getting a hold. Luxuriant potato foliage also shades weeds and limits their growth. Squashes, marrows and pumpkins also offer this shading effect.

Other plant partnerships that are bad news for weeds work because chemicals exuded by the roots of one plant restrict the growth of a neighbour. That is why it is said that you should plant nasturtiums to control couch grass and French marigolds (*Tagetes patula*) to get rid of ground elder and bindweed.

CATCH WASPS IN JAM JARS

And prevent them from getting to your plums and other soft fruit that ripens in late summer. If you discover a wasps' nest in your garden you may need to take more drastic action, or get professional help.

To make a good wasp trap you need a jam jar half filled with sugared or honeyed water and covered with paper with a few holes pierced in it. Lured by the sweetness, the wasps will crawl into the holes and drown. A large plastic drinks bottle makes a good alternative. The best place to site the trap is in a tree.

According to an old German proverb, the better the fruit, the more wasps in it.

A wasp trap may not be enough to save your fruit crop. If you have the energy, fruit on the tree can be individually protected with plastic bags tied over them. The insulation can also help speed ripening.

UNWELCOME TENANTS

It's said that every pair of wasps killed in spring saves the annoyance of a swarm in autumn. Wasps make their nests in roof spaces and wall cavities, as well as in trees and underground, and by late summer a nest can contain up to 5,000 individuals. As long as it is not causing a problem the nest is best left alone until the cold weather arrives and the colony dies away. If it is a problem, you may need professional help to prevent your being set upon by an angry swarm.

Mice love peas

So much so that they may dig up and eat your precious pea seeds. Peas are one of the easiest and most satisfying crops, and worth growing in succession for crops from early summer right through to autumn.

Deep planting will help to deter mice, but it's even better to raise plants in a greenhouse or cold frame. If you are not planning a large crop, individual cells work well. For an entire row, sow the seeds into a piece of guttering filled with soil, then, when the plants are growing strongly, dig a trench in the garden and carefully push in the entire contents of the guttering. You may still have to beware of mice, however.

Mouse deterrents

Coating seeds with paraffin – to deter mice with the smell – was once a widespread practice, as was rubbing them with rosin or coal ashes. Another old gardeners' trick was to cover the ground where peas were sown with several inches of sand, which mice find too unstable for burrowing in. Burying chopped, prickly branches such as those of holly or furze (gorse) is another old

From the reign of George III (1760–1820) it was always the aim in large gardens to have the first crop of peas ready by the monarch's birthday, 4 June.

practice but is not a guaranteed deterrent. For, as Robert Thompson pointed out in *The Gardener's Assistant*, 'mice live snugly enough under furze bushes where old fallen prickles abound'.

CATCH A MOLE IN A TRAP

The old-fashioned trap was one of the more unpleasant ways of ridding a garden of moles, and their molehills, or 'tumps'. Today more humane methods are much preferred, though they may not always be as effective.

The mole (*Talpa europaea*), whose common name is probably a contraction of the charming old name of moldwarp or mouldywarp, is not one of the gardener's friends. As well as creating unsightly molehills, it feeds voraciously on the earthworms that are nature's soil diggers and turners. On the plus side, however, moles will eat pests such as slugs and wireworms. Only rarely seen, the mole makes under-surface tunnel networks that can be as much as 1m (39in) deep, off which it excavates sleeping chambers lined with grass or moss. As the creature digs with its sharp forefeet it pushes earth up to the surface.

A purse made from moleskin will always be full of money.

Every village once had a man who was a mole and rabbit catcher, like the one evocatively described by John Clare:

When melted snow leaves bare the black-green rings,
And grass begins in freshening hues to shoot,
When thawing dirt to shoes of ploughman clings,
And silk-haired moles get liberty to root,

An ancient man goes plodding round the fields
Which solitude seems claiming as her own,
Wrapt in greatcoat that from a tempest shields,
Patched thick with every colour but its own.

The mole catcher was busiest in spring, and mole trapping was a much appreciated country skill.

Advice on using mole traps was often very specific. For anyone using a terrier to catch them, 2.00 am, 6.00 am and 9.00 pm were recommended as the times when the animals are usually at work and when 'heaving up of earth may be noticed'. If traps were used, it was recommended for safety, and to prevent human scent being implanted on the devices, that gloves should be worn at all times.

KINDER ALTERNATIVES

As an alternative to trapping the creatures, the 16th-century gardener Thomas Hyall encouraged boys to play football on his lawns so as to deter mole activity. Today, the preferred means of dealing with moles is to deter them, for instance by filling their runs with gorse, or to create unpleasant noise, such as by burying a wide-necked bottle with its neck just above the soil surface so that the wind blows over it. Moles can be kept away by strong smells such as onions, garlic, eucalyptus or elder leaves, or even urine.

In Britain in 1702, the Jacobites instituted a toast to 'the little gentleman in black velvet', to celebrate the death of William of Orange, who had died in March of that year after a riding accident caused when his horse tripped over a molehill.

Preserve dahlia tubers with sulphur

A good way to kill the destructive diseases that attack the tubers of these garden favourites in winter, even if they are stored in a cool, dry, frost-free place.

Canker and other fungal diseases such as grey mould (botrytis) are the major threats to dahlia tubers over the winter, and bright yellow powdered sulphur is among the oldest and most effective deterrents. After the first frosts, lift tubers carefully and allow them to dry out upside down, so that moisture can drain from the stem remnants. Then sprinkle them liberally with sulphur and place them right way up in straw-filled boxes. Alternatively dip the dried tubers in a proprietary fungicide, dry them again and pack them with their tops (crowns) exposed in peat or sand.

New World ornamentals

Dahlia pinnata, the 'wild' dahlia native to Mexico and cultivated by the Aztecs, was brought to Europe in 1789 by the diplomat Lord Bute, though a plant with double blooms, the cocoxochitl, had been discovered – and accurately illustrated – in the 1570s by Francisco Hernandez, physician to Philip II of Spain. Hernandez had been commissioned to study the 'natural, ancient and political history of the New World'. The dahlia was named in honour of the Swedish botanist Anders Dahl in 1784. Though they come in almost every shape and hue, no one has yet succeeded in breeding a truly blue dahlia.

Sulphur has been used for centuries to combat skin and other human diseases and is the key element in the 'sulfa' drugs discovered in 1935 by the German chemist Gerhard Domagk to be effective against bacterial infections.

DISTURB A CARROT AND YOU'LL GET ROOTFLY

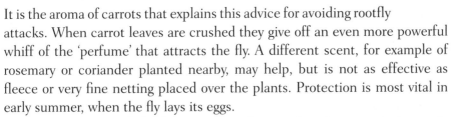

A good reason for sowing seeds thinly to minimize thinning, but not the only way to deter carrot fly, whose maggots burrow into the roots. Prized by cooks for sweet dishes as well as savoury ones, carrots were originally grown as aromatic herbs.

It is the aroma of carrots that explains this advice for avoiding rootfly attacks. When carrot leaves are crushed they give off an even more powerful whiff of the 'perfume' that attracts the fly. A different scent, for example of rosemary or coriander planted nearby, may help, but is not as effective as fleece or very fine netting placed over the plants. Protection is most vital in early summer, when the fly lays its eggs.

Sowing fine seed thinly is not easy. One good trick is to mix the seeds with sand, or even coffee grounds, to spread them out. It is also worth trying a variety billed as carrot fly resistant, such as 'Maestro', 'Primo' or the aptly named 'Resistafly'. Sowing very early, under cloches, so that crops are ready before flies take wing, or after the beginning of summer when their egg-laying season is over, can also help to avoid trouble, as can planting late-maturing varieties such as 'Eskimo'.

Cultivated carrots (*Daucus carota*) are descended from plants native to Europe and western Asia with small, bitter roots. Introduced to Britain during the reign of Elizabeth I they became immediate favourites – so much so that by the time of James I women were wearing carrot tops in their headdresses.

Do carrots really help you see in the dark? Yes they do. Carotene, the orange pigment they contain, is essential to the formation of vitamin A, which is vital for night vision.

Beware the honey fungus

Because it can kill valuable trees and shrubs, including fruit trees, especially apples, pears, cherries, peaches and plums. And because there is no chemical control that will get rid of it, good gardening is the only effective prevention.

Honey fungus (*Armillaria mellea*) is most obvious when, in autumn, clumps of honey-coloured, pale-stemmed toadstools appear at the base of a tree. Just below their caps they have a whitish, collar-like ring. Apart from dieback and general loss of vigour, other symptoms are a sheet of white fungal growth or black strands like shoelaces (rhizomorphs) under the bark. Infected growth can be soft and mushy. Once a plant is in this state there is nothing that can be done but to dig out and burn as much of it as possible. Even this may not prevent further attacks on other trees and shrubs, since the fungus spreads through the soil from plant to plant.

Healthy plants, kept growing strongly with regular feeding, mulching and watering, are less likely to be attacked by honey fungus than those allowed to become distressed by poor cultivation. Spreading flour starch around the tree base to encourage *Trichoderma*, a fungus hostile to the honey fungus, may also help.

For best honey fungus resistance, choose shrubs and trees such as sumachs, kerrias, bamboos, hebes and pittosporums. Apart from fruit trees, avoid willows, currants, lilacs, viburnums and wisterias. And if you cut down a tree in your garden, remove or kill the stump as it can become a natural harbour for the fungus.

On the plus side, honey fungus has an important role in the wild. By breaking down lignum in wood into glucose, which insects can digest, it prevents the world being piled high with the corpses of dead trees.

One year's seed, seven years' weed

Not just an exhortation to get weeds out of the ground before they mature, but testament to the quantity and longevity of the seeds that weed plants produce.

Common annual weeds such as chickweed (*Stellaria media*), fat hen (*Chenopodium album*) and groundsel (*Senecio vulgaris*) are successful because they produce a profusion of seeds that germinate quickly and easily in any soil, maturing to make yet more seeds that do not need months of dormancy before bursting into life again. They are hardy, too, often flourishing through the winter, especially in mild spells. Other seeds, like those of the field poppy (*Papaver rhoeas*), produced by the thousand in a single head, can lie dormant for years until the soil is disturbed, as happened during World War I in the battlefields of Flanders.

Poppies have grown in cornfields since Neolithic times, and it is an ancient belief that they should not be picked as they protect the crops against torrential summer rains.

But annual weeds – especially if hoed from your beds before they set seed – are easy to eradicate compared with perennials. With bindweed (*Convolvulus arvensis*), creeping buttercups (*Ranunculus repens*), horsetails (*Equisetum arvense*) and their like, dogged persistence, if not chemical warfare, is the only way to stop your plants getting choked by their root systems or, with convolvulus, twining stems as well.

It seems strange, since weeds grow so strongly, that someone weak and sickly should be described as 'weedy'.

Useful Weeds

Weeding is a relatively modern concept. Fat hen, now a common weed in vegetable gardens and cultivated fields, thrives on manured ground of any kind and was gathered and eaten from prehistoric times. Until the Elizabethan era, nearly all plants were deemed to have a use of some kind – either as food, medicine or cosmetics. But it is a gardening truth that where there's a root there's a weed. All the more reason for using a systemic weedkiller such as glyphosate as well as all the usual weeding methods.

The endless battle

Age-old views of weeds (which were once thought of as a living metaphor for sin) and weeding:

- *'A really long day of weeding is a restful experience and changes the current of thought.' (Anna Lea Merritt, 1908)*
- *[The gardener] will not suffer a weed to peep up in the garden, while he lets his mind be overgrown with the weeds of vice.' (Wye Saltonstall, 1635)*
- *'The mastery of dandelions is a peculiarly satisfying occupation, a harmless and comforting outlet for the destructive element in our natures.' (Clare Leighton, 1938)*
- *'The sort of weed I most hate ... is the "pusley", a fat, ground-spreading greasy thing, and the most propagatious (it is not my fault if the word is not in the dictionary) plant I know. [But] who can say that other weeds which we despise, may not be the favourite food of some remote people or tribe.' (Charles Dudley Warner, 1876)*
- *'Weeds in paths are a constant worry to those who have not discovered the ghoulish pleasure of using weed-killer ...' (Vita Sackville-West, 1951)*
- *'Weeds want no sowing.' (Old proverb)*

PREVENT CLUB ROOT WITH LIME

A good precaution, but by no means the only way of deterring this fungal disease, which affects all members of the cabbage family and can taint the soil for a decade or more.

With swollen roots, weedy growth and yellowing leaves, a brassica with club root is neither a pretty sight nor a pleasing crop. Lime (see also page 76) is a good preventative because it helps to inhibit the growth of the causative soil-borne fungus *Plasmodiophora brassicae.* After planting out (when a proprietary club root treatment may be applied) it can help to water in with a solution of 500g lime in about 4 litres of water (1lb per gallon).

In addition to keeping soil well composted to help the growth of strong, disease-resistant roots, good crop rotation can also help to eliminate club root. Ideally a seven- or eight-year crop cycle is needed, although in small plots this is unlikely to be practicable.

Before its true cause was identified as a fungus, gardeners believed club root to be caused by maggots, probably because the symptoms are similar to those of gall weevil infestation. An old remedy at transplanting time was to dip roots in a thick mixture of soot and water.

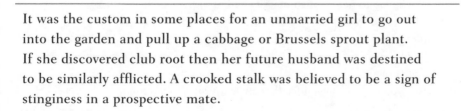

It was the custom in some places for an unmarried girl to go out into the garden and pull up a cabbage or Brussels sprout plant. If she discovered club root then her future husband was destined to be similarly afflicted. A crooked stalk was believed to be a sign of stinginess in a prospective mate.

Keep pond water clean with barley straw

A tried and tested way of controlling the green algal growth that can mar a pond. Rather than sprinkling the straw on to the water, stuff it into an old pair of tights and submerge it, tied to a stake or stout plant, just below the surface.

It is the combination of sunlight and mineral salts in pond water that help algae thrive. Barley straw does not kill them, but it hinders their growth. For maximum effect it needs to be starting to decompose: put it into the pond in early spring and allow at least two weeks for it to exert its effect, and three or four times longer than this if the temperature of the water is below 10°C (50°F). As the summer progresses you can remove the old bundle and replace it with fresh straw.

The added advantage of barley straw is that it is good for pond life. Fish are healthier and studies show that with the straw present and algae absent they are better able to absorb the oxygen dissolved in the water. But never be tempted to substitute hay: not only does it decompose very rapidly, it actually increases algal growth.

Pond tips

More top hints for keeping algae at bay, and your pond in first-rate condition:
- *Regularly scoop off excess algae with a small fishing net.*
- *Plant oxygenating plants such as Canadian pondweed (Elodea canadensis), which help to reduce the mineral content of the water.*
- *Site a pond away from overhanging trees to reduce the number of leaves falling into it.*
- *Avoid splashing lawn fertilizer into the pond, which can massively increase algal growth.*
- *Add water snails, which feed on algae, to your pond fauna.*

Algae – the group that includes the seaweeds – are the simplest of all plants. The earth's first living inhabitants are thought to have been mats of blue-green algae which, by trapping carbon dioxide and producing oxygen, were instrumental in creating the atmosphere that, millions of years later, allowed animals to evolve.

KILL LAWN MOSS WITH SOOT

Or dig it up and use it in your hanging baskets. Soot was a favourite garden cure-all when every home had open fires, and ashes were a popular remedy as well as a useful fertilizer.

Raking or scarifying is the best physical method of ridding a lawn of moss, or you can apply an autumn 'weed and feed' mixture, then rake out the dead thatch in the spring. However, you will never get rid of moss completely unless you address the underlying problem, which is nearly always poor drainage. To improve it, aerate the lawn annually by spiking it with an aerator or garden fork, then top dress it with grit or sand.

Mosses were essential to moss houses, small rustic garden buildings for quiet contemplation, made of wood with moss pressed between the slats. The 18th-century poet William Cowper penned this inscription for a moss house 'in the Shrubbery at Weston':

> *Here, free from riot's hated noise,*
> *Be mine, ye calmer, purer joys,*
> *A book or friend bestows;*
> *Far from the storms that shake the great,*
> *Contentment's gale shall fan my seat,*
> *And sweeten my repose.*

The moss rose (Portulaca grandiflora) is not a rose at all. A succulent annual, this favourite rock garden plant is also known as the sun plant because it closes its petals in dull weather.

To save moss for use in hanging baskets or as a mulch, spread it out on a tray and wait for it to die off, during which time it will darken in colour.

6. WHATEVER THE WEATHER

It must be more or less true that on every day of the year gardeners are anxious about the weather, simply because of its effects on the progress of their flowers, fruit and vegetables. So it should be no surprise that many old sayings and pieces of advice hinge on the jobs best done at particular times of year and on the effects of sun and rain, wind and weather. In the past, many of these were directly related to the year's festivals and saints' days, which is why, for example, it is traditional for gardeners to plant potatoes on Good Friday and to have peas and beans in the ground by St David's Day, 1 March.

Despite the vagaries of the weather, and though the trend of the climate is towards warmer winters, the seasons roll around from year to year with little major variation. So while gardeners need to wait until the soil is warm to plant out vegetable seeds, and to keep tender plants under cover until the risk of frost has passed, the plants themselves are in fact able to make sense of, and respond to, the yearly round, which explains why daffodils bloom before tulips, roses are the flowers of high summer, and chrysanthemums are the beauties of the autumn.

There is an old Chinese proverb averring that 'rain in spring is as precious as oil', and we gardeners of today are much more concerned with water shortages than were our forebears. While wet summers will surely never be totally a thing of the past, wise gardeners should do as much as they can to conserve rainwater in every season.

SPRING IS SOONER RECOGNIZED BY PLANTS THAN BY MEN

A fact that long pre-dates the findings of plant physiologists, namely that plants respond naturally to the lengthening days that herald the spring, putting out new growth and coming into bloom.

While many in northern temperate regions count 1 March as the first day of spring, the 'official' start of the season is 21 March, the vernal equinox. The weather can be very variable, and March is said to 'come in like a lion and go out like a lamb'. But, as Samuel Beeton's 19th-century *Dictionary of Every-Day Gardening* reminds us, 'Every day of genial weather imparts strength and inspires confidence, and a number of flowers, either in embryo or further advanced, greet us with their gladdening look of beauty.'

As bulbs begin to come into flower, and primroses and pulmonarias open, the garden takes on a wonderful freshness, even in early spring, though after a hard winter it may look rather bedraggled in parts. It is wise not to cut back any perennials yet, as their growth will still give protection against frosts.

If your soil is light and chalky, early spring is a good time for digging and manuring. Although an old saying runs: 'In October manure your field/And your land its wealth shall yield', on light soils winter rains can leach out much of the manure's goodness.

'Slayer of the winter, art thou here again?
O welcome, thou that bring'st the Summer night!
The bitter wind makes not thy victory vain
Nor will we mock thee for thy faint blue sky.
Welcome, O March! Whose kindly days and dry
Make April ready for the throstle's song,
Thou first redresser of the winter's wrong!'
William Morris, *The Earthly Paradise*, 1868

Whether the Weather Be Snow or Rain, We Are Sure to See the Flower of St Faine

A tribute to the fact that gardeners can rely on the evergreen *Viburnum tinus*, commonly called the laurustinus, to be in flower on 1 January.

The large, flat heads of this viburnum's attractive pink flower clusters begin to open – usually paling to pale pink or white as they do so – from late autumn onwards. Though it has smaller flowers, the variety 'Variegatum', with creamy yellow margins to its leaves, is also well worth a place in the winter garden.

The laurustinus was a great favourite in the Victorian shrubbery. Writing in *A Flower for Every Day* in 1965, Margery Fish remarked, 'If this were any way a difficult plant we should pay far more attention to it. As it is so easy it often gets the worst positions in the garden.' She recommended that because it makes such a lovely sight – 'its happy way of crouching into a corner with its voluminous growth spread gracefully around' – it is best used as a specimen shrub or as a superb natural hedge. Other good deciduous viburnums for winter colour include the bronze-leaved *V. farreri* and *V. x bodnantense* 'Dawn', with flowers whose heady fragrance is unsurpassed. Like all viburnums they do best in moist soils in sun or dappled shade.

As well as being New Year's Day, 1 January is the feast of St Faine or Fanchea, who persuaded her brother, the Irish prince Enda, to renounce his dreams of conquest and found Ireland's first monastery. He too was sanctified.

Snowdrops are the Fair Maids of February

Snowdrops are truly the heralds that promise the return of spring. These February fairmaids, closely linked with ancient church traditions, still grow naturally in profusion at many monastic sites.

Hardy once established, snowdrops like plenty of moisture during their growing period (helped by lots of humus). The bulbs can be planted in mid-autumn, but results are more reliable if the plants are lifted, divided and moved immediately after flowering. Apart from the 'ordinary' snowdrop (*Galanthus nivalis*), there are many interesting varieties to choose, such as the full double *G. nivalis* 'Flore Pleno', the autumn-flowering *G. reginae-olgae* and the almond-scented *G. allenii*.

In country districts snowdrops are commonly called Candlemas bells, as the feast of Candlemas falls on 2 February. It marks the purification of the Virgin Mary, which fits well with the snowdrop's symbolic spotlessness. On that day it was the custom for young girls, dressed in white, to strew bunches of snowdrops on the church altar – from which the image of the Virgin had been removed.

The cousin of the snowdrop is the larger snowflake or *Leucojum*, which is also sometimes known as the 'high snowdrop'. Snowflakes of different species flower in varying seasons and are named accordingly – *L. vernalis* in spring. *L. aestivum* in summer and *L. autumnale* in the autumn.

> Other names for the snowdrop include Mary's taper (another reference to the Virgin) and, for obvious reasons, snow piercer and dingle-dangle.

THERE IS A HEATHER FOR EVERY MONTH OF THE YEAR

Certainly there is, though only if you have acid soil or are prepared to grow your heathers in containers or raised beds, and can keep their soil well drained. Fortunately, most winter-flowering heathers are totally tolerant of chalky, alkaline soils.

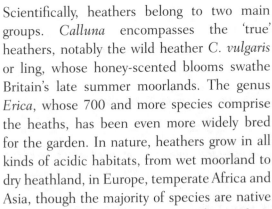

Scientifically, heathers belong to two main groups. *Calluna* encompasses the 'true' heathers, notably the wild heather *C. vulgaris* or ling, whose honey-scented blooms swathe Britain's late summer moorlands. The genus *Erica*, whose 700 and more species comprise the heaths, has been even more widely bred for the garden. In nature, heathers grow in all kinds of acidic habitats, from wet moorland to dry heathland, in Europe, temperate Africa and Asia, though the majority of species are native to the Cape Province of South Africa. There is also a third, small genus, *Daboecia*, which includes the lavender-flowered St Dabeoc's heath.

Bees love heather and the plants will attract them to your garden. Heather honey is prized for its superior taste and in hives set on a heather moor a single colony can make as much as 15kg (33lb) of honey in just two weeks.

If your heathers need watering, avoid tap water, which is likely to be alkaline. As with azaleas, the ideal is rainwater collected in a butt. Keep plants well trimmed to stop them becoming straggly. Prune summer-flowering types in spring, the remainder after flowering.

Heathers have many traditional uses. Like gorse, they were once used for everything from cattle fodder and bedding to thatching roofs and making brooms. The flowers were used for making sweet tisanes, ales and beers, and as the source of an orange dye. Heather is particularly associated with Scotland, and it was the Scots who took *Calluna* to America, where it quickly became naturalized, as remarked in this verse by the 19th-century American poet John Greenleaf Whittier:

> No more these simple flowers belong
> To Scottish maid and lover,
> Sown in the common soil of song
> They bloom the wide world over.

White heather found by accident in the wild, if given as a gift, is believed to bring good fortune to both giver and receiver. A sprig is often added to a bride's bouquet.

AN ALL-YEAR HEATHER SELECTION

Within each of these species, you can choose from varieties in almost every shade of pink, crimson, cream and white.

Erica carnea (alpine or winter heath)	Late autumn–mid-spring	Lime tolerant and hardy
Erica australis (Spanish heath)	Mid-spring–early summer	Not lime tolerant. Prone to wind and snow damage
Erica cinerea (bell heather)	Early summer–mid-autumn	Needs acid soil
Erica vagans (Cornish heath)	Midsummer–mid-autumn	Vigorous
Calluna vulgaris (ling)	Midsummer–late autumn	Needs acid soil
Erica manipuliflora	Early autumn–late autumn	Lime tolerant and hardy
Erica x darleyensis	Early winter–mid-spring	Suitable for all soils

SOW PEAS AND BEANS ON DAVID AND CHAD, BE THE WEATHER GOOD OR BAD

An instruction to be sure to have seeds in the ground by St David's Day on 1 March or the festival of St Chad the day after. Though this admonition is fine for peas and broad beans, for other types of beans the gardener needs to give more thought to the weather.

This sowing timetable is reinforced by another old gardener's rhyme, which runs: 'Be it weal or be it woe, Beans should blow before May go,' implying that by the end of May plants should be growing and well established. Another verse demands attention to other signs of spring (and knowledge of the sizes of pre-decimal British coinage):

> Plant kidney beans, if you be so willing,
> When elm leaves are as big as a shilling,
> When elm leaves are as big as a penny,
> You must plant beans if you mean to have any.

Daffodils are worn on St David's day, but leeks are also closely associated with it. According to legend, Welsh warriors battling against the Saxons in the seventh century wore leeks in their hats to show which side they were on. In fact leeks may not have reached Britain until the 1500s, and the vegetables may well have been ramsons or wild garlic.

All this is fine as long as the soil is not cold and damp, which will make even the most resilient peas and broad beans rot away and will certainly put paid to more tender French and runner beans. Outdoors and unprotected, French and runner beans will not germinate successfully until late spring, though strong plants, ready to set out once the risk of frosts is passed, can be obtained from seeds sown a month earlier under cloches, fleece or in a greenhouse.

PLANT POTATOES ON GOOD FRIDAY

The efficacy of this advice depends on where you live and the timing of Easter. In southern England, for example, a crop is believed to be doomed if planted on that day, but in the North, and in the Midlands, where Good Friday is known as 'Spud Day', the reverse is true.

Because Easter is a movable feast – it falls on the first Sunday after the first full moon following the vernal equinox (21 March) – planting potatoes on Good Friday will not guarantee either good weather or warm soil. Advice concerning the moon and potato planting is contradictory, at best, but majority opinion favours planting when the moon is on the wane (which chimes with Good Friday) but also in darkness before the moon rises or after it sets. For a very early crop, ready to eat by Christmas, buy specially prepared potatoes and plant them in midsummer, using fleece to keep off the frosts. These can also be grown in large pots or specially made 'gro-sacs' and brought into a cool greenhouse in autumn.

Some country folk still believe that carrying a potato in your pocket will draw out from the body the substances that cause rheumatism.

During World War II the new potato was 'illegal' in Britain. To get the maximum yield from the crop, commercial growers were forbidden to lift their potatoes before 21 July, and amateur gardeners were asked to do the same.

WHEN YOU CAN TREAD ON NINE DAISIES AT ONCE, SPRING HAS COME

Or three, or a dozen. The saying varies from family to family. These pretty 'earthbound stars' as the poet Chaucer called them, can be seen in flower nearly all year but burst into a profusion of blooms in spring.

The daisy is named in two ways. Its common name comes from 'day's eye', referring to the fact that it opens at dawn to reveal a flower with a miniature sun at its centre and closes its pink-tinged petals at sunset. It generic name, *Bellis*, comes from the Latin for beautiful – its specific epithet, *perennis*, refers, botanically, to its perennial nature.

As well as lawn daisies, which are far from universally appreciated by gardeners, there are many cultivated varieties bred from the common daisy, such as the double white *Bellis perennis* 'Alba Plena', the large double crimson-flowered 'Rob Roy' and the semi-double pink 'Alice'. *Bellis rotundifolia* 'Caerulescens', though not predictably hardy, is worth growing for its single flowers with beautiful pale purple petals and vivid yellow centres.

He loves me, he loves me not.

In cricket, a daisy cutter is a ball that reaches the batsman rolling along the ground. It is named from the fact that the plant's rosette of leaves lies flat to the ground – where it is also beyond the reach of mower blades.

PROTECTIVE POWERS

The ox-eye daisy, which can often be found growing wild as a garden 'escape', is a flower that is sacred to St John and is used in midsummer ceremonies on St John's Eve, 23 June, particularly as protection against thunder and lightning. With other plants, including St John's wort, ivy, elder, foxglove and thyme, it was picked and fumigated in the traditional St John's Eve bonfire, then hung up in the house and in cow stalls to give year-round protection against everything from disease to supernatural evil.

CULTIVATED CHOICES

Other than Bellis there are many daisy-like flowers that will earn their place in the garden. All are members of the family Compositae.

- **Helichrysum** – the 'petals' of these flowers are in fact dry, papery bracts, giving them the alternative name of everlasting flowers because they last for months after being cut. H. frigidum is an evergreen sub-shrub.
- **Anthemis** – a genus of hardy annuals and herbaceous perennials.
  A. tinctoria is the golden marguerite and A. punctata ssp. cupaniana is low growing and ideal for rock gardens. It also has aromatic foliage.
- **Leucanthemum** – easy-to-grow, usually white-flowered daisies with single or double flowers. L. vulgare is the marguerite or ox-eye daisy, and L. x superbum is the shasta daisy. L. paludosum is a dwarf species best cultivated as an annual.
- **Boltonia asteroides** – a herbaceous perennial with loose flower clusters in white or purple with bright yellow discs.
- **Erigeron** – the fleabane. Species and varieties come in a range of yellows and oranges as well as white. E. glaucus is pale violet.

Oak
BEFORE ASH,
ONLY A SPLASH ...

... ash before oak, soak, soak, soak. This rhyme, long used to predict the summer weather from the order in which these two trees come into leaf, is not a very reliable guide as the ash almost always comes second.

Britain's Woodland Trust, using records going back to the 18th century, confirms the dubious worth of the rhyme. Bearing its delicate sprays of tufted flowers before the leaves emerge, the ash is rarely in leaf before the oak. However, British summers are getting hotter and drier, so it may be premature to write off the forecast altogether.

The English oak (*Quercus robur*) can live for well over five hundred years and reputedly as long as a thousand, and many named trees appear as landmarks on old maps. If your garden is big enough, an oak is a wonderful heirloom tree to plant and, if you have the patience, can be reared from an acorn. However, you may want to choose a smaller species such as the pretty semi-evergreen willow oak (*Q. phellos* syn. *pumila*) or, for autumn beauty, the scarlet oak (*Q. coccinea*).

QUEEN OF THE FOREST

The ash (*Fraxinus excelsior*), easy to recognize in winter from its black buds and silver-grey bark, is sometimes called the Queen of the Forest and in Scandinavian mythology was Yggdrasil, the tree of life. A tree of this type will severely rock the foundations of a house or wall if planted too close, and can be more of a curse than a blessing when its winged seeds germinate in every bed, nook and cranny. The manna ash (*F. ornus*), native to southern Europe, bears superb heads of fluffy, scented, creamy-white flowers in early

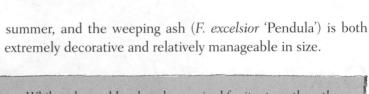

summer, and the weeping ash (*F. excelsior* 'Pendula') is both extremely decorative and relatively manageable in size.

While oak wood has long been prized for its strength as the weight-bearing timbers of houses and ships, ash combines both strength and elasticity, and is still the wood of choice for making crab and lobster pots. Ash is also prized as firewood, as it will burn when green, hence the saying: 'Ash dry or ash green makes a fire fit for a queen.'

APRIL SHOWERS BRING FORTH MAY FLOWERS

In northern temperate regions, the garden will come to life in May whatever the weather the previous month, but it is a fact that a dry April is not conducive to plant growth.

The uncertainties of spring weather keep gardeners on their toes, as grass begins to grow strongly, weeds start to flourish and seeds of summer vegetables need sowing. It is not too late to prune and feed roses, and they will benefit greatly from watering if the weather is dry.

In the vegetable garden, it was once the custom to time plantings by the arrival of migratory birds. In Cheshire, for instance, it was thought risky to plant potatoes until the yellow wagtail had been seen – hence the bird's nickname of 'potato dropper'. In other places the cuckoo gave the signal for potato planting, as in the rhyme:

*When you hear the cuckoo shout
'Tis time to plant your tatties out.*

If you have a garden pond, be prepared for a noisy April, as frogs and toads call to their mates. You may also be able to use frogs to predict the weather, as in the saying 'the louder the frog the harder the rain'.

RAIN IS FAR MORE IMPORTANT TO GARDENS THAN SUN

Not a new observation, but one that is increasingly true given the trend towards hotter, drier summers. All the more reason to grow drought-resistant plants in the garden, and to use water with care.

Plants love rain, especially persistent, gentle 'growing rain', as opposed to massive downpours that flatten plants as they over water them. And although rain can keep less hardy gardeners indoors, most would concur with the sentiment expressed by Margaret Waterfield in 1907: 'More and more I am coming to the conclusion that rain is a far more important consideration to gardens than sun, and that one of the lesser advantages that a gardener gains in life is the thorough enjoyment of a rainy day!'

After a long, hot spell, even a thunderstorm can be welcome. Writing of such an experience in 1900, Gertrude Jekyll marvelled at the transformation of a garden 'in pitiable state of dirt and suffocation'. Waking in the night she welcomed the sound of the rain, knowing 'that the clogged leaves were being washed clean' and in the morning was happy 'to see how every tree and plant is full of new life and abounding gladness'.

Drought makes plants suffer and wilt, as they lose more water from their leaves than they can absorb from the soil. Precious water is best given to the garden early in the morning or late in the day, when water loss is least. Succulent plants, which retain water in their fleshy leaves, always do well in dry weather, though they may not survive frost. Among annuals, the least thirsty types include antirrhinums, cosmos, petunias, fuchsias and clarkias.

IS IT GOING TO RAIN?

Gardeners hoping for rain – or not – have long relied on signs of nature to help predict it. Old country signs of a wet summer are rooks building their nests low in the trees and ash trees in leaf before oaks (see page 177). Of the animal signs you may look for, the most reliable is swallows flying low – because their insect food flies nearer the ground when the air is moist. Far less reliable are cows lying down in the fields, cats washing over their ears or sheep walking about and bleating.

PRECIOUS WATER

Top water-saving tips:
- *Collect rainwater in a butt (ideally connected to a roof).*
- *Save and use 'grey water' – the water used to wash vegetables, bath water (dilute soap solution will help kill aphids) and water collected from defrosted freezers. Avoid water containing softening salt or large amounts of detergent.*
- *Compost and mulch thoroughly when the soil is damp for best possible water retention.*
- *Add water-retaining granules to the compost when filling pots and baskets.*
- *Don't worry about the lawn. Even if it turns brown it will quickly revive once it rains again.*
- *Sink 'watering spikes' next to vulnerable plants so that any water you give will go directly to the roots. This is especially useful for small, newly planted trees and shrubs.*
- *Plant salad vegetables close together and cover them with fleece, which helps to trap moisture.*
- *Site thirsty plants in full or partial shade, where they will lose less water through transpiration from their leaves.*

Beware of frosts in May

Late frosts can kill tender plants overnight and spell ruin for the flowers of fruit trees. Wary gardeners do well to listen carefully to the weather forecasts in spring and protect plants if necessary.

In northern temperate regions, May frosts are common. Rather than hoar frosts, which leave a white rime on plants, May frosts are usually black frosts, so called because plants freeze during the night then turn black when the sun melts their sap in the morning. It is the sudden expansion that occurs on warming, not the cold, that is the killer. In the vegetable garden, frost is not always fatal. Potatoes will often make a remarkable recovery, and crop well.

If your garden is in a frost pocket – a valley particularly prone to frost – choose late-flowering varieties of fruit or frost will kill your blossom and decimate your crop. A wise gardener will keep tender plants such as dahlias, busy lizzies, squashes and lettuces in the shelter of a conservatory, greenhouse or cold frame until all risk of frost is past. Though it may not look particularly pretty, fleece draped over plants such as passion flowers, or vulnerable fruit trees with flowers in bud, is a good solution.

In the country, cold weather in May is referred to as the 'blackthorn winter', because the blackthorn or sloe is in flower in the hedgerows. Saints whose feast days fall at this time – St Mamertus on 11 May, St Pancras on 12 May, St Servatius on 13 May and St Boniface on 14 May – are traditionally known as the 'frost saints'.

SET SAGE IN MAY AND IT WILL GROW ALWAY

Late spring is certainly a good time for planting sage and all kinds of perennials and shrubs. The Romans regarded sage as sacred, and by the Middle Ages it was seen as a cure-all, good for treating everything from digestive ailments to rheumatism and even memory failure.

May is the month that the garden comes to life, and healthy plants quickly establish themselves. It is a good month to take cuttings of thyme, rosemary and pot marjoram, as well as sage itself. To ring the changes with the common sage (*Salvia officinalis*) try the varieties 'Tricolor', whose leaves are splashed in pink, white and purple, the purple and green-leaved sages of the Purpurascens Group, and 'Icterina', whose leaves are green, gold and pale yellow. For best results, and to keep plants vigorous and bushy, site sage in full sun. In spring, trim it back but be careful not to cut into the old wood or you may precipitate its demise.

SAGE IN THE KITCHEN

Common sage was used by both the Greeks and Romans as a robust flavouring that married perfectly with strong meat. With onions, it is still key to a classic stuffing for pork or goose. For a milder effect, some cooks prefer Greek sage (*S. fruticosa*) or, for desserts, the pineapple sage (*S. rutilans*) or the lavender sage (*S. lavandulifolia*).

Sage has been used since ancient times to make a herbal tea that is believed to strengthen the muscles, protect against diseases, including plague and epilepsy, and deter nightmares.

Sage leaves are believed to be an excellent ant deterrent.

A SWARM OF BEES IN MAY IS WORTH A LOAD OF HAY ...

... A swarm of bees is June is worth a silver spoon. A swarm of bees in July is not worth a fly. In other words, by late summer the value of the swarm is minimal.

Honeybees swarm in order to increase their numbers. Around the end of spring or in early summer the young queens are ready to fly from the hive or from colonies established in old buildings or hollow trees. At the same time the worker bees become restless: they can be seen gathering at the hive entrance, then going back inside again to raid the honey cells for food.

When a new queen emerges, about half the workers first cluster, then swarm around her as she flies off. If she has already been impregnated by a drone, the swarm will seek a new home. If not, it may return to the hive it has just left, in which case any remaining unfertilized queens will be killed by the workers.

During the summer a colony of honeybees (*Apis mellifera*) consists of about 50,000 workers (sterile females), a few hundred drones (males) and one queen. The workers make the honey that sustains them all, which they feed to the queen and drones over the winter. Of the 200kg (440lb) or more that a colony may produce, only about a third is used by the bees. And the better use the swarm makes of the profusion of early summer flowers, the more honey there will be.

'How doth the little busy bee
Improve each shining hour
And gather honey all the day
From every opening flower!
How skilfully she builds her cell!
How neat she spreads the wax!
And labours hard to store it well
With the sweet food she makes.'
Isaac Watts, *Divine Songs for Children*, 1715

CHERRY BLOSSOM IS THE CELEBRATION OF SPRING

Whether grown for their fruits, or simply for their magnificent flowers, cherry trees are one of the most heartening sights of spring. While greatly welcomed everywhere, they are especially celebrated in Japan.

Although described as 'cherries', some of the spring ornamentals are in fact peaches, apricots and plums, but they all display their blossoms against bare branches, and many have the additional virtue of fabulous autumn leaf colour. From the many species and varieties it should be easy to find one to suit your garden. Because they can react badly to pruning – which can even kill them – they are best cut back soon after flowering when they are still in vigorous growth, rather than during winter dormancy.

In Britain cherry blossom can be found in the wild as well as in the garden. The wild cherry (*P. avium*), also called the gean, or in some places the mazzard, bears drifts of white blossom in spring and is equally attractive in autumn when its foliage turns to fiery yellows and crimsons. The dark brown bark, which peels to reveal patches of deep red, adds to the tree's attractiveness. When cut, the trunk exudes a resin which, in country places, has long been used as a type of chewing gum.

> On St Barbara's Day, 4 December, it was a Czech tradition to cut cherry boughs and keep them indoors so that they would bloom on Christmas Eve. Girls would secrete the blossoms under their clothes when they attended midnight Mass – and the boys would attempt to find and steal them.

JAPANESE TRADITION

The flowering of the cherry blossom is an event for celebration in Japan, where families take time off to view the blooms and honour them with parties and picnics, in a custom known as *hanami*. Japanese meteorologists report daily on the movement of the *sakura zensen*, the warm 'cherry blossom front' that brings the mild weather the trees need to flower.

An abundance of flowers

Whether you prefer your blossom pink, white or even red there is a tree to fit your preference. Some top Prunus choices include:

P. padus	Bird cherry	Flowers small, white, almond scented
P. persica	Ornamental peach	Pale rose-pink flowers
P. tenella	Dwarf Russian almond	Flowers bright pink
P. cerasus	Sour cherry	White flowers in dense clusters
P. 'Okame'	Ornamental cherry	Blooms in deep carmine
P. mume 'Bene-chidori'	Japanese apricot	Fragrant pink flowers

WHEN THE SCARLET PIMPERNEL CLOSES IT'S GOING TO RAIN

Not for nothing is this small, bright red flower known as the poor man's weatherglass, change-of-the-weather, shepherd's sundial and weather flower. It will invariably close its petals if the sky becomes overcast ahead of rain.

The scarlet pimpernel (*Anagallis arvensis*), a common weed of gardens, waste ground and dunes, is not, however, an all-day forecaster. Whatever the weather, it will have closed its petals by 2.00 pm and will keep them shut until 8.00 am. If the petals open fully in the morning a fine day

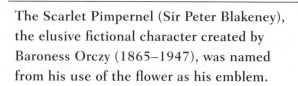

The Scarlet Pimpernel (Sir Peter Blakeney), the elusive fictional character created by Baroness Orczy (1865–1947), was named from his use of the flower as his emblem.

can be expected. But the reverse is not true. When the flowers fail to open first thing it is likely to remain cloudy, but the chance of rainfall is little better than about 15 per cent.

Like the scarlet pimpernel, other flowers, including daisies (*Bellis* spp) and bindweeds (*Convolvulus* spp) close when the air is damp because the cells at the base of the petals detect and respond to increasing levels of moisture. When they close later in the day the petals are responding to lowering levels of sunlight.

STOP PICKING ASPARAGUS ON THE LONGEST DAY

The logic behind this good advice is to give asparagus plants plenty of time to renew their underground resources before the onset of winter. By chance, the longest day coincides with the end of the six-week cropping season for asparagus.

Asparagus is easy to grow as long as you have the patience to wait for the crowns to mature, since even spears from three-year-old crowns (roots) should not be cut for two years. But given good drainage, fertile soil and an annual top dressing of compost, a healthy bed can last for two decades and more. Growers in the past would bury animal horns, especially those of sheep, to help keep their asparagus beds fertile.

The asparagus plant is a kind of lily, probably cultivated since Egyptian times. It was a favourite of the ancient Romans, and Pliny the

Elder described asparagus grown in Ravenna as so large as to be 'three to the pound'. Male and female flowers are borne on different plants. Though it makes no difference to the crop, choosing all male plants will stop the spread of the seedlings that can sprout in profusion from fallen berries.

Asparagus is prone to attack from the orange and black asparagus beetle, which is attracted by the plant's distinctive smell. This same smell can taint the urine within an hour or two of eating asparagus.

> The name 'sperage' was commonly used in English in the 16th and 17th centuries, and was later changed to 'sparrow grass'. Growers and market traders still know asparagus as 'grass'.

A WET SUMMER BRINGS ON TOMATO BLIGHT

The fungi that devastate an outdoor tomato crop flourish most in wet weather, and the warmer it is the worse the problem. What's more, the spores linger in the soil from year to year, making blight notoriously hard to eradicate.

A tomato plant infested with blight is a sorry sight. Blackened leaves hang limply from its weakened stem, while those fruits not already rotting on the ground below are brown or blackened with the fungus. The only thing to do is to collect all the infected material and either burn it or dispose of it with general household waste.

Because the spores do not rot it should never be composted. Blight is as hard to prevent as it is to eradicate. Fortnightly spraying with Bordeaux mixture (made from copper sulphate and hydrated lime) may work before and during attacks, but is far from foolproof. Growing your tomatoes indoors or on a patio is the best way to avoid blight.

> The tomato (Lycopersicon lycopersicon), a native of the Americas, was first cultivated by the Aztecs, who named it tomatl, meaning 'plump fruit'. The tag of 'love apple' comes from its 16th-century reputation as an aphrodisiac, hence the Latin poma amoris, the French pomme d'amour and the Italian pomodoro.

In July, let herbs you would preserve run to seed

As well as providing you with valuable seeds, the aromatic oils in the leaves will become concentrated as the plants age.

Dill (*Anethum graveolens*), coriander (*Coriandrum sativum*) and fennel (*Foeniculum vulgare*) are the trio of garden herbs easiest to grow for their seeds, and all respond favourably to a well-drained, sunny site. All are simple to cultivate from seed (which you can save yourself) sown in mid-spring, or when the soil has warmed up. When the seed heads mature they can be cut off and hung upside down to finish drying. The seeds can then be shaken out and stored in airtight containers.

Caraway (*Carum carvi*), which is a little trickier and needs warmth and shelter, can also be added to the collection. It is a biennial, so you need to sow a year before you want to harvest, and it produces a large, thick root (which can also be eaten).

In the kitchen, both dill and fennel (which has a more pronounced aniseed flavour) are perfect partners for fish. Dill seeds are also a key flavouring of the pickled cucumbers traditional to Nordic cuisine. Coriander seeds go into curries and oriental dishes, while the flavour of caraway seeds typifies ryebreads, old-fashioned 'seed cake' and liqueurs such as the German Kümmel.

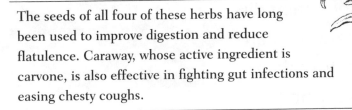

The seeds of all four of these herbs have long been used to improve digestion and reduce flatulence. Caraway, whose active ingredient is carvone, is also effective in fighting gut infections and easing chesty coughs.

BE ACTIVE IN AUGUST FOR A COLOURFUL SPRING

And a productive one. A wide variety of seeds can be sown in late summer and will happily overwinter. This is also a good month for striking a whole variety of cuttings.

In the flower garden, seeds of both wallflowers (*Cheiranthus cheiri*) and sweet williams (*Dianthus barbatus*) are ideal subjects for late summer sowing, and both will survive well outdoors if plants are well established before the frosts begin. It is also not too late to sow biennial and perennial stocks (*Matthiola* spp), especially Brompton varieties. For the best sweet peas (*Laythrus odoratus*) it is the practice among show winners to germinate seed in late summer or early autumn, then overwinter plants in cold frames.

Choose shoots from your best pelargoniums for cuttings now, setting them into a mixture of compost and sharp sand. This is also an excellent month for rose cuttings, as the warmth of the season will help them take. If you need to keep them outdoors, a good tip is to place them under shrubs for protection, then keep them well watered and undisturbed until the following autumn.

Grow your own manure: sow seeds of red clover in late summer, then dig in the plants as a green manure, before they flower, in spring.

VEGETABLES TO SOW IN LATE SUMMER

Lettuce – *choose a variety that has been bred for overwintering, such as 'Valdor' or 'Winter Density'.*

Radishes – *continue regular sowings, and keep the plants well watered.*

Spring cabbage – *select a hardy variety such as 'Dorado'.*

Radicchio – *don't sow earlier than this or it will run to seed. Even if the outer leaves get frosted, the hearts will keep well until spring. It appreciates protection with fleece.*

Rocket – *will stand well over the winter except in the most severe frosts.*

Spinach – *choose a variety such as 'Triathlon' for crops in late autumn and spring.*

Pak Choi – *will overwinter in mild areas if well protected.*

Kohlrabi – *will last until spring if sheltered with fleece or cloches.*

THE CHRYSANTHEMUM IS QUEEN OF THE AUTUMN

Dubbed a 'serviceable flower' by Muriel Spark's fictional Miss Jean Brodie, the chrysanthemum has probably been in cultivation in China since before 500 BC, though it is now associated even more strongly with Japan.

That the chrysanthemum is out of place earlier in the year was the view of the English gardener Margery Fish, who wrote in *A Flower for Every Day* that 'chrysanthemums belong to autumn and their scent conjures up bonfires and fallen leaves'. So, she added, 'I do not take kindly to chrysanthemums in July; on the other hand I would be very pleased if I could persuade some of my favourites to bloom before the end of October – or even later.'

Like other showy autumn flowers, chrysanthemums have an inbuilt means of detecting that the hours of daylight are getting shorter, which stimulates them to flower. The easiest to grow are the hardy

For some years the generic name of the garden *Chrysanthemum* was changed to *Dendranthema*, but this has now been officially reversed. New varieties are constantly being bred, among them the strange Saga-giku varieties or spider chrysanthemums, whose elongated petals look like spiders' legs.

outdoor chrysanthemums, including the small 'Charm' types (the earliest to flower and also excellent as pot plants) and those of the Rubellum group, which will grow to about 1m (3ft). So-called florists' chrysanthemums can be grown outdoors or, for late flowering, they may be raised in the greenhouse.

For the best blooms

Although 'Charm' chrysanthemums are easy to grow from seed, most autumn-flowering outdoor types are best propagated by cuttings that are taken in early spring and hardened off in a cold frame before planting out. To control the number and size of blooms, disbudding is essential. For spray chrysanthemums, remove the topmost bud and allow the side shoots to develop. For the largest possible single blooms, allow only the top bud to remain. All but the hardiest varieties will need to be dug up and stored in a frost-free place over the winter.

In an informal garden, there are still few chrysanthemums to beat the Korean or 'cottage garden' types. From the few varieties now available two of the best are 'Ruby Mound', which bears its large double ruby-red flowers throughout late summer and autumn, and the silvery-pink 'Emperor of China'. If grown in a crowded border these 'mums' do not usually need staking, though they will benefit from support if placed in a windy spot.

Chrysanthemum symbolism

- Since the 14th century the chrysanthemum has been the national flower of Japan, and the 16-petalled chrysanthemum was the emblem of the Mikado.
- For Japan's Festival of Happiness, also known as National Chrysanthemum Day, the flowers are displayed in houses, shops and temples.
- The Supreme Imperial Order of the Chrysanthemum, Japan's highest honour, awarded 'for meritorious service to the Japanese nation', was founded by Emperor Meiji in 1876.
- After his death in the fifth century the home town of the Chinese chrysanthemum breeder T'ao Yüan Ming was changed to Chu-hsien, the City of Chrysanthemums, in his honour.
- To give a chrysanthemum with a message, choose the colour carefully. White means 'truth', red 'I love you' and bronze 'friendship – but not love'.

September blow soft till the fruit's in the loft

This country plea for good weather at harvest time strikes a sympathetic note with the gardener. Today we are more likely to store our fruits in the freezer, but old-fashioned jams and preserves are still popular.

High winds in early autumn are especially damaging to the apple crop, tearing good fruit from the trees and turning them into bruised windfalls that quickly rot. For apples to keep well, perfect health is essential, for even if they are individually wrapped in oiled paper and kept from touching each other by being placed in moulded cardboard fruit trays, it is easy for the spores of rot-producing fungi to move from one apple to the next. Hence the reason for needing to beware of 'one bad apple in the barrel'.

Frugal cooks will peel, chop and generally find a host of ways to rescue the best of their windfalls, but will also relish whole apples kept through the winter. These are best picked from a ladder, each one tested by placing a hand under it and simultaneously lifting and twisting. If the fruit is ripe it will come away easily and can then be carefully placed in a basket.

As a rule, late season apple varieties such as Laxton's Superb and Bramley's Seedling are better keepers than early ones.

A HOT SUMMER MAKES FOR AUTUMN COLOUR

For deciduous trees and shrubs, the brilliance of autumn is indeed enhanced by hot weather earlier in the year, but it may be short-lived if the year is dry. Whatever the weather, New England is renowned – and much visited – on account of the intensity of its autumn colours.

While leaves appear green in summer, the green pigment chlorophyll masks various other pigments, including anthocyanins and carotenoids. These, though they make themselves obvious only in autumn, are produced in maximum quantities at high temperatures. So when, as the summer ends, chlorophyll begins to break down, the underlying colours become apparent. The more anthocyanins the leaves contain, the redder they will be. A mixture of anthocyanins and carotenoids gives orange autumn colours, while carotenoids alone make for yellow leaves.

AUTUMN CHOICES

For reliable autumn colour in the garden, few trees can beat the Japanese maples, such as *Acer palmatum*, whose leaves turn a fabulous scarlet-orange. If you have room for it, the field maple *A. campestre* will give you bright yellow leaves. For a red-purple choose *Cornus kousa,* and for copper brown, *Taxodium distichum*. On walls, few plants surpass the crimson of *Parthenocissus tricuspida*, the Virginia creeper, and for yellow *Hydrangea petiolaris* is good.

It is an old belief that an abundance of autumn berries is a sign of a cold winter to come, but it's more likely to be a sign that there has been a good summer.

Lose no time in November

Though late autumn weather can vary from mild and wet to freezing cold, a dry, crisp day is perfect for clearing up and preparing the ground for the year to come.

Leaves to sweep ... tulips and trees to plant ... roses to move ... perennials to tidy ... soil to dig – this is indeed a busy month. New tulip bulbs can be

Know your tulips

Tulips are categorized into 15 divisions. Early types flower in early and mid-spring, otherwise all are late spring flowering.

1 **Single Early** *Short-stemmed. Good for forcing.*
2 **Double Early** *Taller than the single early tulips with full, lush petals.*
3 **Triumph** *Tall and ideal for bedding. Dozens of varieties.*
4 **Darwin Hybrids** *Among the tallest, usually in shades of red and yellow.*
5 **Single Late** *Also tall. Includes Darwin and Cottage tulips.*
6 **Lily-Flowered** *Long, curvaceous flowers with pointed petals like the original Turkish tulips.*
7 **Fringed** *Flamboyant flowers with fringed petals, sometimes edged in a contrasting colour.*
8 **Viridiflora** *Green-streaked flowers.*
9 **Rembrandt** *Single flowers with stripes or streaks. Now nearly obsolete.*
10 **Parrot** *Profusely cascading petals that curl in all directions, named for the shape of the flower buds.*
11 **Double Late (Peony Flowered)** *Flamboyant heads, full of petals.*
12 **Kaufmanniana** *The 'water-lily tulips' with long, slender petals that open flat in the sun. Very early flowering.*
13 **Fosteriana** *Tall, slim flowers, with glossy green or grey-green foliage. Early flowering.*
14 **Greigii** *Rigid stems and medium-sized flowers that flare out dramatically in the sun, with striped or mottled leaves.*
15 **Species** *Includes early and later flowering types. Good for naturalizing.*

planted out, as well as those you have lifted and kept from the previous year. By waiting until late autumn you will ensure that they do not start to sprout too quickly in mild spells.

Plants that need winter protection should by now be indoors, and crops such as parsnips and beetroot that you plan to leave in the ground should be covered with straw or fleece to prevent frost damage. This is the ideal time to plant bare-rooted trees and to move shrubs.

If the weather is mild, weeding and even mowing may still be essential tasks. If it is cold and wet, begin planning what seeds you will need for next year, clean and sterilize empty pots, clean and service the lawnmower and get the shears sharpened.

PLANT GARLIC ON THE SHORTEST DAY AND HARVEST IT ON THE LONGEST

A good way of saying that garlic will survive the winter and produce its crop in summer. In fact cloves can be planted at any time from mid-autumn, and are better put in well before the ground is cold and hard with frost.

Individual cloves taken from a single head of garlic (*Allium sativum*) and pushed no more than 5cm (2in) into the soil will provide a dozen or more plants. Underground, the single clove multiplies itself into a complete new head. By midsummer's day, or soon after, when the top growth begins to die down, you can start eating the new season's crop. Known as 'wet garlic', it has a wonderfully mild flavour. For keeping, pull up the heads, dry them off for about two weeks, then hang them in strings in a cool dry place to use throughout the winter.

Although garlic likes to be kept well watered in spring during dry spells, wet weather can make it vulnerable to white rot, a fungal disease that destroys the bulbs. It is almost impossible to treat, and experts say that following such an infection plants of the onion family should not be grown on the soil for eight years.

GENTLER FLAVOURS

Those who prefer a milder taste may like to cultivate elephant or Russian garlic (*Allium ampeloprasum* var. *ampeloprasum*) which, as its name suggests, has extremely large cloves. Botanically this is actually a close relation of the leek, not a true garlic. Tribute to its palatability is the fact that garlic ice cream and garlic 'chips' are all served at the annual Elephant Garlic Festival in North Plains, Oregon. Even 'ordinary' garlic will become sweet and mild if cloves are slow-roasted in their skins.

GARLIC LORE

In Egyptian tombs, garlic was left as an offering to the gods. In the Bible, the Israelites during their exodus complained about having to eat manna, saying: 'Remember how in Egypt we had fish for the asking, cucumbers and melons, leeks and onions and garlic.' In folklore garlic has long been attributed with the ability to keep at bay both evil spirits and vampires. Pliny said that, in the presence of garlic, a magnet would lose its attractive powers.

Planting a garlic crop near susceptible crops is a good way of deterring attacks from greenfly, blackfly and other garden pests, though by no means infallible. A garlic spray may be more effective (see box, page 153.)

Eating three raw cloves of garlic a day has been proven to improve men's fertility.

KALE IS WINTER'S MOST VALUABLE VEGETABLE

Although much denigrated as 'what cows eat', kale – also known as collard greens – is a valuable and nutritious winter vegetable valued since the times of ancient Greece and Rome. In Scotland, the word 'kail' was once synonymous with 'dinner'.

Although common or garden kale has curly leaves, the type most prized in Italian cooking is the dark-leaved Tuscan kale called *cavolo nero*. It is thought that kale was originally favoured in Mediterranean countries because, unlike cabbage, it could survive hot weather. It is extremely hardy and tolerant of frost, which is why gardeners were advised (especially in wartime) not to use it until other vegetables became scarce. Furthermore, by cutting off the tops of the plants but leaving the stems intact, plenty of side shoots can be encouraged to grow.

The leaves of kale, also known as borecole, are rich in both iron and vitamin C. Of the green varieties, curly kale has the best flavour. Coloured types have been known since the 18th century, when Richard Bradley, writing in *The Country Housewife and Lady's Director* in 1732 of what he called 'coleworts', remarked that they are of 'various Colours, such as Reds of all Sorts, Purples, Yellows and Greens, and also White. I have seen a bed of these,' he continued, 'as beautiful as ever I saw any Thing of the Garden.'

Once the crop was over, the hard, woody stems of kale, in country districts, were sometimes dried and used as walking sticks.

Index

netting 74, 83, 139, 159
nettles 94, 136, 137
New England 194
newspaper 15, 122
night-scented stocks 12
night vision 159
nitrogen 94, 105, 136, 137
notebooks 33
Nôtre, André Le 129
Novello, Ivor 116
November 195–6

oak 177, 178, 180
Odysseus 56
oil of lavender 125–6
onions 144, 146
onion hoes 134
opium 62
orchids 32
oregano 101
Organ Fountain 27
overwintering 108, 152, 189, 196
ox-eye daisies 176

Paeon 53
pak choi 87, 190
Pancras, St 181
pansies 67
paper-bark maple 114
paradise 11
paraffin 152, 155
Parkinson, John 37, 53, 59, 125–6
parsley 98, 101
parsnips 87, 196
paths 21–2
Paxton, Joseph 28
peas 155–6, 173
peaches 73
pears 73, 78–9, 111
pelargoniums 64–5, 67, 189–90
penstemons 60–1, 142
peonies 53
perennials 63, 68, 69
  deer-proof types 142
periwinkles 52, 142
perry 79
Persephone 91
Persia 11, 26
pests 139–46, 148–50, 152, 154–7, 159
Peter Rabbit 139
Peter the Great, Tsar 29
petunias 67, 180
pH 76
philadelphus 121, 128
Philip II, King 158
phlox 122
phosphates 137
phosphorus 137
photosynthesis 58
Phytophthora 147
pieris 15
pigeons 83
Pilgrim's Way 118
pinching out 93, 108, 152
pinks 15, 54, 55
pittosporum 160
Plasmodiophora brassicae 163
Pliny 40, 78, 82, 122, 129, 186–7, 197
plum 111
pollen 32, 50, 83, 149
pollen beetles 149–50
pollination 92, 149
polystyrene 31
ponds 26, 179
  algae control 164
Popeye 89
poppies 35, 61–3, 122, 161
Portland, Isle of 139
potash 105, 136
potassium sulphate 96, 136
potatoes 76, 86, 99, 146, 153–4, 174, 178
potato vines 142
pots
  drainage 31
  keeping small 64
Potter, Beatrix 139
pricking out 17–18
primroses 50
primulas 67
privet 32
Prosperine 62
pruning
  clematis 118
  forsythia 120